T0328765

Cambridge Elements

Elements in the Philosophy of Law
edited by
George Pavlakos
University of Glasgow
Gerald J. Postema
University of North Carolina at Chapel Hill
Kenneth M. Ehrenberg
University of Surrey

SOCIOLOGICAL APPROACHES TO THEORIES OF LAW

Brian Z. Tamanaha
Washington University School of Law

CAMBRIDGE
UNIVERSITY PRESS

CAMBRIDGE
UNIVERSITY PRESS

University Printing House, Cambridge CB2 8BS, United Kingdom

One Liberty Plaza, 20th Floor, New York, NY 10006, USA

477 Williamstown Road, Port Melbourne, VIC 3207, Australia

314–321, 3rd Floor, Plot 3, Splendor Forum, Jasola District Centre,
New Delhi – 110025, India

103 Penang Road, #05–06/07, Visioncrest Commercial, Singapore 238467

Cambridge University Press is part of the University of Cambridge.

It furthers the University's mission by disseminating knowledge in the pursuit of
education, learning, and research at the highest international levels of excellence.

www.cambridge.org
Information on this title: www.cambridge.org/9781009124362
DOI: 10.1017/9781009128193

First published 2022

A catalogue record for this publication is available from the British Library.

ISBN 978-1-009-12436-2 Paperback
ISSN 2631-5815 (online)
ISSN 2631-5807 (print)

Sociological Approaches to Theories of Law

Elements in the Philosophy of Law

DOI: 10.1017/9781009128193
First published online: May 2022

Brian Z. Tamanaha
Washington University School of Law

Author for correspondence: Brian Z. Tamanaha, btamanaha@wustl.edu

Abstract: This Element applies empirical insights to examine theories of law proffered by analytical jurisprudents. The topics covered include artifact legal theory, law as a social construction, idealized accounts of the function of law, the dis-embeddedness of legal systems, the purported guidance function of law, the false social efficacy thesis, missteps in the quest to answer "What is law?" and the relationship between empiricism and analytical jurisprudence. The analysis shows that on a number of central issues, analytical jurisprudents assert positions inconsistent with the social reality of law. Woven throughout the Element, the author presents a theoretically and empirically informed account of law as a social institution. The overarching theme is that philosophical claims about the nature of law can be tested and improved through greater empirical input.

Keywords: analytical jurisprudence, artifact legal theory, law as a social construction, what is law, functions of law

ISBNs: 9781009124362 (PB), 9781009128193 (OC)
ISSNs: 2631-5815 (online), 2631-5807 (print)

Contents

1 Introduction

Analytical jurisprudents have asserted that law is a type of social institution, law is a social artifact or social construction, law maintains social order, law guides and coordinates social behavior, law enforces social and moral norms, law is an instrument of social control, and law is an instrument that serves social purposes. Legal positivist theorists assert that law is based on social sources, social facts, and social conventions. "What then is an account of the nature of law, of its essential properties? We are trying, I have suggested, to explain the nature of a certain kind of social institution," Joseph Raz observed. "This suggests that the explanation is part of the social sciences" (Raz 2009a: 23). Legal philosopher Andrei Marmor put it emphatically: "[L]aw is, profoundly, a social phenomenon" (Marmor 2007: 36).

Since law is a social phenomenon, it would seem to follow that theories of law have much to learn from the social sciences. H. L. A. Hart asserted that his classic book, *The Concept of Law*, "may also be regarded as an essay in descriptive sociology" (Hart 1961: v). In various aspects of his work, he appeared open to input from the social and natural sciences. His incorporation of the internal point of view of rules referred to Peter Winch's argument that rule-based social behavior must be apprehended internally (Hart 1961: 242; Winch 1958). As Winch put it, social action is intelligible within "ways of living or modes of social life" that social investigators must apprehend in order to understand what people are doing and why (Winch 1958: 100). In his argument that all societies have basic rules about persons, property, and promises necessary for group survival, Hart considered naturalistic causal explanations (Hart 1961: 189–207). "Causal explanations of this type do not rest on truisms nor are they mediated by conscious aims or purposes; they are for sociology or psychology like other sciences to establish by the methods of generalization and theory, resting on observation and, where possible, on experiment" (190). Despite these scattered entreaties to the sciences, however, Hart maintained that analytical jurisprudence is an autonomous approach grounded in philosophy (Postema 2015: 876–77), and he generally dismissed sociology as scientifically weak (Lacey 2006: 950–53). "Hart was relatively impervious to historical and sociological criticism, precisely because he saw his project as philosophical and therefore immune to the charge of having ignored issues that seem central to historians and social scientists" (953).

Following Hart's lead, prominent contemporary analytical jurisprudents have shown little interest in the social sciences. Joseph Raz opined, "Sociology of law provides a wealth of detailed information and analysis of the functions of law in some particular societies. Legal philosophy has to be content with those few features which all legal systems necessarily possess" (Raz 2009b: 104–5). "Social science cannot tell us what the law is because it studies human society," declared Scott Shapiro. "Its deliverances have no relevance for the legal philosopher because it is a truism that nonhumans could have law" (Shapiro 2011: 406, n. 16). Analytical jurisprudent Michael Giudice acknowledged that "Shapiro's view is in many ways an amplification of a theme (or vice) found in many statements of the goals and methods of analytical legal theory" (Giudice 2020: 9). Philosophy of law, in their view, involves conceptual analysis grounded on intuitions and purported truisms, which does not require social scientific studies of law.

As Gerald Postema remarks:

> Law is a complex social phenomenon linked with other social phenomena that structure the lives of human beings who have certain distinctive capacities, are limited by certain weaknesses, and driven by certain needs, principal among them the need to live together. We might likewise observe that the specific shape law might take in any historical community of human beings may vary with differences in the social, political and natural circumstances in which they live, and that these variations themselves vary over time. These are not theoretically partisan thoughts, but common starting points for philosophical reflection on law for more than two millennia; not hard-won theoretical wisdom, but just common sense.
>
> Yet contemporary analytical jurisprudence often seems to ignore them.
>
> (Postema 2021: 1)

Against this general orientation, increasing signs have appeared of openness to input from the social and natural sciences, along with the recognition that legal philosophy must account for law as historically conditioned and interconnected with society. Gerald Postema, Michael Giudice, Keith Culver, Frederick Schauer, Dan Priel, Kenneth Ehrenberg, Brian Bix, and Brian Leiter, among other analytical jurisprudents, have advocated greater attention to the social sciences and the social reality of law. Recently, a handful of experimental studies and surveys have been conducted on jurisprudential matters. Whether this represents a marginal development or a fundamental shift toward analytical jurisprudence becoming more empirically informed remains to be seen.

Sociological Approaches to Theories of Law applies an empirically grounded perspective drawing on the social and natural sciences to examine key issues on theories of law proffered by contemporary analytical jurisprudents. The primary thrust of this Element is critical, with a constructive aspect woven through the analysis. The critical thrust demonstrates that on a series of central issues, analytical jurisprudents assert positions that are inconsistent with the empirical reality of law. Given the concision of the Cambridge Elements series, these criticisms are necessarily selective. The main focus is on positions asserted by analytical legal positivists. Many issues are omitted; a limited number of theorists are addressed; and the discussion of each issue is truncated. I expose problems with theories about law as an artifact, idealized accounts of the functions of law, the claim that law guides social conduct, the social efficacy thesis, the purported supremacy of law, the conflation of law with legal system, the view that law is a singular phenomenon with essential features, and other issues. These critical examinations are intended to prompt analytical jurisprudents to reexamine various central points about law. More generally, this critical engagement is offered to demonstrate the philosophical benefits of greater empirical input.

The constructive aspect presents a thoroughly social perspective on law. The discussion of law as a social construction, which largely draws on the work of George Herbert Mead, articulates what is entailed in viewing law as a social institution. "The standpoint taken is that law is through and through a social phenomenon; social in origin, in purpose or end, and in application," as John Dewey put it (Dewey 1941: 76). Hence, "'law' cannot be set up as if it were a separate entity, but can be discussed only in terms of the social conditions in which it arises and of what it concretely does there" (77). This is why analytical jurisprudence cannot operate as an insulated, autonomous philosophical enterprise.

My theoretical view of law has been elaborated in other work (Tamanaha 2001, 2017, 2021). A few basic propositions are set forth here. Law is subject to natural human traits and the requirements of living within social groups. Law is a historical product interconnected within society that develops in relation to surrounding cultural, social, economic, political, legal, technological, and ecological factors. These influences are internal as well as external to society, for no society develops in isolation, particularly in an increasingly interconnected world. These influences seep through law in every pore, and law influences society in ways that are mutually constitutive, interactive, and dynamic. Manifestations of law vary across societies – with various core commonalities – and have evolved over time to take on different forms and functions. Modern legal systems operate through highly specialized knowledge, norms, practices, and institutions maintained by legal professionals. Law reflects moral norms, but law can also be captured by groups, advancing certain views and interests over others, clashing with prevailing norms and interests. Law is an instrument that serves the ends of those who influence, shape, enlist, invoke, and wield it. Not only does law resolve disputes, but it is also often embroiled in social, economic, and political conflicts. This is a realistic understanding of law in action.

To avoid misunderstandings, I should make my position clear up front. I avidly read analytical jurisprudence and find much of the work edifying. The argument I press is *not* that analytical jurisprudence should become sociological, nor that philosophical questions about law can be fully taken over by the sciences. My contention is that analytical jurisprudents will produce sounder theories of law when they take it upon themselves to seek empirical input on the philosophical issues they contemplate. A number of pivotal theoretical assertions, as I show, rest on empirical claims or assumptions that lack support. Philosophical accounts of what law is, what law does, how people conceive of and utilize law, what the consequences of law are, and so forth must be better informed empirically.

2 The Problems with Artifact Legal Theory

Contemporary legal philosophers theorize law on two distinct tracks: social artifacts and social constructions. On the former track, Jonathan Crowe stated, "It is often stated that law is an artifact" (Crowe 2014: 737). Brian Leiter considers it incontestable that "The concept of law is the concept of an artefact, that is, something that necessarily owes its existence to human activities intended to create that artefact" (Leiter 2011: 666). On the latter track, Leslie Green observed, "We might say [laws and legal systems] are social constructions" (Green 2012: xvii). "Contemporary philosophy of law is often characterized in terms of its central debates, yet such debates have not prevented an apparent consensus from emerging: law is a social construction," Giudice remarked (Giudice 2020: 1; Priel 2019). These assertions prompt the question: Which theoretical framework is best suited for law? They are not interchangeable: all artifacts are social constructions, but social constructionism is far more expansive and multidimensional than artifact theory.

This section critically examines artifact theories of law by its main proponents, Jonathan Crowe, Kenneth Ehrenberg, Luka Burazin, and Corrado Roversi. I show that artifact legal theory suffers from multiple problems and distorts legal phenomena in order to meet the strictures of the theory. The objections I raise to artifact legal theory are analytical and sociological. As philosopher Dave Elder-Voss observed, "any plausible social ontology must also be consistent with a plausible complex of sociological theory" and "with empirical evidence" (Elder-Voss 2012: 20). The following section articulates the social construction of law, filling out what this means, demonstrating that it provides a far richer and more adequate account of law.

Artifact theory has been a hot topic in philosophy in the past couple of decades. "An artifact may be defined as an object that has been intentionally made or produced for a certain purpose" (Hilpinen 2011; Preston 2018). The builder of a chair, for instance, intentionally makes it with the appropriate material and structure so that people can use it to sit on. Amie Thomasson, a leading artifact theorist, summarizes: "Artifacts are standardly treated as mind-dependent entities, since for an artifact to be created, there must be fairly structured intentional states, involving an individual intending to make a thing of a certain sort, with certain intended properties – and also, of course, being relatively successful at executing those intentions" (Thomassen 2014: 54). Philosophical accounts of artifacts typically identify three requirements: artifacts are (1) intentionally created, (2) functional objects, and (3) the intended function determines what kind of artifact it is (46). To encompass art as an artifact, Thomasson drops the necessity to show an intended function, instead requiring that it be "intentionally created and successfully endowed with certain intended features – intended features that may, but need not, include an intended function" (57). Artifact kinds, then, can be categorized through the intended features/functions.

The assertion that law is an artifact is odd in several respects. Legal rules, institutions, and systems are not obviously *intentionally* constructed *objects* by *authors or creators* with a *particular purpose or function or set of features*. To make this framework fit, artifact legal theorists must loosen the meanings of, and the connections between, authors, intentions, objects, features, and functions. Luka Burazin writes, "Since in principle no one person creates a legal system from scratch, since usually a legal system has no precisely identifiably authors, and since it seems that many people with different roles over a long period of time contribute to the emergence of and continuous existence of a legal system, it seems that the artifact theory of law should adopt a very broad concept of authorship" (Burazin 2016: 399). Corrado Roversi acknowledges, "Now, to be sure, these solutions require to a certain degree that the concept of artifact be 'stretched' – something that some may not be ready to accept" (Roversi 2019: 58). An obvious conclusion from these difficulties is that the artifact framework is ill-suited for law, but artifact legal theorists nonetheless strive to make it work.

The first move by artifact legal theorists is to shift from material objects to abstract institutions, enlisting John Searle's social ontology, particularly his notion of collective recognition. Searle reduces the logical structure of society to three core ideas (Searle 2006). First, *assignment of function*: humans assign functions to objects. For example, pieces of paper with certain markings are used for buying, selling, and storing value (the functions of money). Second, *collective intentionality*: we-intentionality involves a cooperative sense of doing something together (unlike the self-focus of I-intentionality). In a game of football or an orchestra, each player understands that their part connects with others to create a whole (a football play or a symphony). And third, *constitutive rules*: constitutive rules create certain activities, institutions, and institutional facts (regulative rules only regulate activities but do not create them), usually in the form *"X counts as Y in context C"* (Searle 2006, 2010). X is an object, person, or entity; "counts as" involves collective acceptance; Y is a status with deontic powers carrying "rights, duties, obligations, requirements, permissions, authorizations, entitlements, and so on" (8–9); and C is the situation in which these collectively recognized powers attach. A cut of paper with certain dyed markings (X) counts as money (Y) when it is printed by the Bureau of Engraving and Printing and circulated (C). Searle adds a fourth idea to supplement these three, what he calls the Background for intentional action, which I elaborate on later.

This account has clear applications to law. A particular set of words in rule form (X) is legally binding (Y) when duly enacted by the legislature, signed by the executive, and officially registered (C). Legislatures and courts are organizations composed of people holding offices with collectively accepted statuses carrying legal deontic powers. Certain individual people (X) are collectively recognized as possessing legal authority (as legislators, judges, prosecutors, police, etc.) (Y) when duly appointed and acting in their official capacities (C). People recognize that the police have the power to arrest, prosecutors to prosecute, legislators to legislate, judges to judge, and jailors to jail. This collective recognition (which at least involves going along with) exists within the community as well as among the legal officials themselves. (This general account will be modified later.)

Artifact legal theorists use Searle's theory in various ways to demonstrate that law is an artifact. To account for customary law, Jonathan Crowe drops the intention requirement for artifacts, relying on collective acceptance, arguing that customary law is an unintentional artifact (Crowe 2014: 743–48; Priel 2018). To his credit, Crowe does not stretch the notion of intentionally, acknowledging that it does not work for customary law. Standing in the way of his approach, however, is the strong consensus among philosophers that intention is a defining feature of artifacts. Moreover, once the intention is dropped, there is no conceptual reason to retain artifact theory rather than social constructionism, which incorporates but is not strictly wedded to intentional creation, as the following section explains.

Ehrenberg, Roversi, and Burazin present law as an intentionally created artifact in relation to different legal "objects": specific laws, legal doctrines and legal institutions, and legal systems (law as such). Their analysis also applies to legal organizations, which artifact legal theorists have largely ignored, though I draw out for critical purposes. At the outset, it bears emphasis that artifact legal theory squeezes an extraordinarily diverse range of phenomena within the same artifact box. Artifact legal theory, according to Ehrenberg, postulates "seeing law as an artifact type, albeit an abstract one, in the same way we think of shoes, hammers, hospitals, universities, and corporations" (Ehrenberg 2016: 47). This statement is unintentionally revealing. Any theory that lumps together such radically diverse phenomena must be exceedingly thin, with little content and information value.

The easiest case for artifact theorists is *individual laws* declared by courts and legislatures, although this application faces daunting difficulties. When enacting a law, legislators may have no single or shared intention about the meaning or purposes of the law they enact. Trial and appellate courts, furthermore, may issue interpretations of a law that differ from the intentions of the legislators. Appellate courts regularly issue plurality decisions in which individual judges on a panel articulate separate, inconsistent justifications for supporting the outcome (see Tollefsen 2002), and appellate courts regularly disagree among themselves on the interpretation of the same law (called circuit splits in the USA). On top of that, court interpretations can change over time owing to changing views of judges or to changing circumstances. All of these scenarios can occur with respect to a single law: legislators voting for it may have differing yet coinciding intentions; members of an appellate panel with differing yet coinciding intentions may interpret it in ways that were not intended by the majority of legislators; and different appellate courts may interpret said law in different ways concurrently and over time.

So what (or which) is the intentionally created law artifact, and who are its creators? It is not clear whether *the* intentional artifact is the words in the statute understood through the original purpose (assuming arguendo a single purpose exists) or whether new artifacts are created each time judges subsequently give it new meaning and new purposes (while the words of the statute remain unchanged). Keep in mind, moreover, American jurists who adhere to textual interpretation of statutes and original public meaning interpretation of the US Constitution deny that the intentions of those who enact the law control how it should be interpreted – what matters is the meaning conveyed by the terms of the law.

Consider the US Constitution. Who are the creators/authors of the US Constitution: the individual drafters who wrote specific provisions, the delegates who voted for it at the Constitutional Convention, the state voters who ratified it, or all of them in the aggregate? There are manifold inconsistencies among these various creators/authors about the intended meanings and purposes of the constitutional provisions they enacted. Is the Commerce Clause – which authorizes federal legal powers – a single artifact? The meaning and scope of this provision have changed enormously over time through court interpretations in connection with social, economic, political, technological, and legal changes across two-plus centuries. Does each interpretation that alters its meaning create a new Commerce Clause artifact?

Artifact legal theory faces formidable problems identifying author(s), object(s), and intended purposes or features(s) with respect to particular laws. For these troubles, no evident conceptual illumination or advance is achieved by characterizing individual laws as artifacts. The sole insight artifact theory produces is that people with legal powers intended to create, interpret, and apply a given law with some purpose in mind. Not only is it obvious, but also, even worse, it is misleading because it obscures the multiplicity of intentions and purposes, and changes, in connection with individual laws.

Laws and doctrines that constitute *legal institutions*, like property or marriage, are far more complicated than individual laws. There are two senses of property: type and token. Property is a legal institution constructed by legal doctrines (an institutional type); John Smith's ownership of Blackacre is a specific instance of property (an institutional fact or token). Anglo-American land law (setting aside personal property and intellectual property) involves a broad array of rules. These property rules evolved over centuries, influenced by origins in feudalism and customary law, as well as by changing economic and political circumstances and clashes between contesting interests – involving barons, the landed gentry, the merchant class, farmers and ranchers, miners, serfs and renters, city dwellers, and so on (see Simpson 1986). Land law has been shaped by power, ideology, changing technology, the industrial revolution, and the rise of urbanization. In addition, land law interacts with and has been shaped by past and present chattel law, tort law on trespass and nuisance, contract law on leases, succession law, trust law, mortgage law, zoning law, modern aviation (which altered air rights over land), mining and water rights, and sanitation and environmental regulations. Innovations in property doctrine, furthermore, are often created by lawyers in the service of clients, with the intention to seize and control assets, secure income streams, and engage in rent-seeking (Pistor 2019). Particular instances of property disputes – should a delinquent tenant be evicted during a pandemic? – are subject to a variety of legal and policy considerations. A continuously evolving assortment of rules by innumerable creators with no single, joint, or characteristic intention or purpose, Anglo-American land law is not a single abstract institutional type. Incrementally changing over time through statutes, judicial modifications, and creative lawyering, property is a multiplicity, as reflected in competing positions in the philosophy of property (Katz 2018).

Corrado Roversi's historical-intentional model of legal institutions purports to account for this "by tracing artifactuality to a historical property rooted in an original 'creative process' consisting of authorial intentions and in a series of further modification, reinterpretation, and development processes"; so legal institutions are "the outcome not just of an original authorial intention but also, and more significantly, of a history of intentions" (Roversi 2019: 51). This presents legal institutions like property as *singular* "objects" formed originally, and at each moment thereafter, by a purportedly determinative intention, washing away the continuous process of conflicting intentions, clashes over the contours of the property, fluid shifts, and inconsistent property doctrines. Property is a contested patchwork of internal heterogeneity with aspects intentionally created and other aspects incidentally (unintentional by-products) resulting from interaction with other bodies of law and surrounding factors (economic, ecological, etc.). Roversi analogizes legal institutions like property to a Gothic church constructed on the remains of a Roman temple that consists of contradictory design plans (Roversi 2018: 104, 2019: 58); but the church is still a singular fixed object, whereas property (and other legal institutions) is more akin to a shape-shifting bricolage multiplicity.

The contention that *law* or *legal system* is an artifact is the most problematic of all. The objections raised previously apply to legal systems as well, but here, I focus on the inability of artifact legal theorists to establish that creators *intentionally* create legal systems as *objects* with specified *features/functions*.

Ken Ehrenberg claims law (as a genre or type) is an artifact kind, which includes as subsets legal enactments, legal decisions, and legal systems. It is "correct to think of legal system as an exemplar of law as a genre" (Ehrenberg 2016: 5, n. 11). To identify the intended function of law, he asserts, one must identify the intended functions of individual laws, from which he generalizes to identify the function of law as a genre. Ehrenberg explains: "[B]y seeing law as a kind of artifact, we are imagining that those who create individual enactments do so with an intention in mind about what the enactment is to accomplish. We then hope to gather those functions together and characterize them in a general way as much as possible in order to understand law as an institution" (27, 138, 144).

Identifying the intention behind legal enactments is not the same as the intention behind legal systems. Here is how Ehrenberg ties them together: "[L]egal systems are often self-consciously designed to be frameworks for the creation of individual laws" (17), or alternatively, evolved legal systems emerge as a by-product of making laws. Since the intended function of laws is coordination and to generate institutions, he asserts, and legal systems produce and apply laws, the *intended function of legal systems is coordination and the generation of institutions.* Thus, Ehrenberg reasons parasitically from the fact that legal systems create laws, to generalize that their function is identical to the function of the aggregate of individual enactments.

When discussing legal rules, legal organizations, and legal systems, one must be careful to avoid either of two fallacies that involve the relationship between parts and wholes. A fallacy of composition is committed if one assumes that since the function of legal rules is to coordinate behavior, therefore, the function of legal organizations or legal systems is to coordinate behavior; a fallacy of division is committed if one assumes that since the function of legal systems is to coordinate behavior, therefore, the function of individual legal rules is to coordinate behavior. Wholes and parts can have the same function, but this must be established with respect to each, not simply extrapolated from one direction or the other.

Legal enactments and legal systems are distinct, each (according to artifact legal theory) with its own intentional set of features and/or functions (cf Burazin 2019a: 230–31, 234). A critical difference is that specific legal enactments occur pursuant to concrete intentions (albeit mixed), whereas many existing legal systems evolve over centuries in connection with surrounding factors with no overall constitutive intention. That was Searle's position: "[E]xcept for special cases where legislation is passed or the authorities change the rules of a game, the creation of institutional facts is typically a matter of natural evolution, and there need be no explicit conscious imposition of function" (Searle 1995: 125).

The fact that several different levels of purported legal "artifacts" are involved, with different respective intentions, can be drawn out via Ehrenberg's repeated references to "institutions like hospitals, universities, and legal systems" (2016: 47, 75, 2018: 184, 190). Notice that the items on this list are not parallel: A legal system is not like a hospital or university. Legal system is parallel to health care system and higher education system. A hospital is a particular bureaucratic *organization* with the purpose of providing medical treatment to sick and injured people (2016: 8–9). Parallels within law to a hospital as an organization is a courthouse, a legislature, a prosecutor's office, a police department, a law firm, and so on, each of which has its own orientation, purposes, and constitutive rules, manifested in the intentions and actions of the people who comprise them. *Legal systems* are *not organizations.* Legal system is an abstraction, a label used to encompass many differentiated organizations, each with its own characteristic knowledge, practices, intentions, and purposes.

To put the differences in sociological terms, specific laws and judicial decisions are created at the *micro* level (particular situations of action); courts and legislatures operate at the *meso* level (organizations); and legal systems are at the *macro* level (large scale phenomena). Micro phenomena are the easiest to link to constitutive intentions, and meso phenomena are often undergirded by intentional actions, but many macro phenomena are not intentionally created as such. Artifact legal theorists must keep each distinct, tying purported intentional creation to each, because in artifact theory intentions determine the features/functions of artifacts. Burazin offers a direct account of the intentional creation of legal systems, which I take up in a moment.

First, let us examine the function of law identified by Ehrenberg. His book extensively analyzes various theories of law and accounts by legal theorists, including Dworkin; natural law; legal positivism; and so on (though it bears mention here that legal theorists are not intentional creators of laws or legal systems) (Ehrenberg 2016: 180–91). Drawing on these theoretical accounts, he presents two functions. "[O]ne primary function of law is to solve coordination problems" (197). Artifact theory reveals the second function: "The contribution of seeing law as a kind of institutionalized abstract artifact adds to the list the function of setting a framework for the specification, recognition, and protection of contextually bound rights and duties within the widest possible social setting (setting them apart for a particular kind of emphasis), that is, the generation and validation of other institutions" (197). Put more simply, the function of law is to generate other institutions (36). The two functions are compatible, he says, in that creating institutions is an aspect of law's coordination function (197).

Ehrenberg's identification of law's function departs from artifact theory and does not follow his own proposed method of generalizing law's function from individual legal enactments. Instead, he builds on accounts of the function of law *by theorists*, accounts which were not themselves based on generalizing from *actual* intentions ("in mind") of those who create individual laws. This is a crucial deviation. Since the creator's intention about function is causally tied to the artifact created, "we generally expect that it is the *intention of a creator that assigns artifacts their function*" (Ehrenberg 2016: 51, emphasis added). "The imposition or assignment of function is simply the use of an object to fulfill a purpose" (Ehrenberg 2020 282, describing Searle's account). Makers of chairs know people must be able to sit on what they make and build them to serve this function.

When engaged in making law, judges and legislators typically do not consciously intend to solve coordination problems. Instead, they focus on the content of the law and its various implications and consequences (political, legal, economic, cultural, etc.) – *that* is "the intention in mind about what the enactment is to accomplish" (Ehrenberg 2016: 27). When enacting the Affordable Care Act, the expressed intention of legislators was to expand medical insurance coverage – not to solve coordination problems. When deciding whether the liability of manufacturers for injuries to consumers caused by their products should be based on strict liability or negligence, judges' intentions aimed at what they viewed as the correct outcome considering social, economic, fairness, and legal factors and consequences – not at solving coordination problems. Legislators engage in negotiations with other legislators and consult powerful constituencies, while the legislative staff actually draft the legislation (legislators in the USA regularly do not actually read the full bills they enact into law, which can run to many hundreds of pages). Judges process cases, hold hearings, and decide particular motions that apply law to the facts, and so on, work they divide up with law clerks. While engaging in legal activities, rarely do legal actors consciously think about creating the legal system or its features and functions. Legal officials and actors are immersed in and occupied with immediate legal tasks. Solving coordination problems is the intended purpose of law where coordination is the primary concern (like traffic laws), but modern courts and legislatures issue a limitless array of laws and decisions for a multitude of purposes, the vast bulk of which are designed to achieve particular objectives at hand. The coordination function of law is a *generalization of legal theorists*, who Ehrenberg relies on for his account, but is not what legal officials actually intend when they create and apply laws.

Here is the main objection in a nutshell: artifact theory for objects invokes genuine intentions, whereas artifact legal theorists project nonexistent, unknown, or unknowable intentions with respect to law in order to satisfy the requirements of artifact theory. They speak of the intentions of the creators of each law, legal institution, and legal system past and present, including evolved versions that originated before memory and records, akin to a fictitious original state of nature. Writing about collective intentionality, philosopher Deborah Tollefsen pertinently observes: "[B]oth the summative and nonsummative accounts of group intentionality overlook the fact that our attributions of intentional states to group members are often made in ignorance of the actual intentional states of the members" (Tollefsen 2002: 29). Although Ehrenberg rejects latent functions as inconsistent with artifact theory, it turns out that his attribution of coordination and the creation of institutions as the intended function smacks of latent functions, since these particular purposes are not in the minds of lawmakers when creating laws (more about latent functions later).

Luka Burazin differs from Ehrenberg in linking intention specifically to the creation of the legal system. "According to the artifact theory of law, legal systems are abstract institutional artifacts. They are artifacts since they are created by authors who have a *particular intention to create the institutional artifact 'legal system '*" (Burazin 2016: 397, emphasis added). Burazin adds that the community addressed by the legal system must collectively recognize their legal authority and largely comply with the norms (Burazin 2016, 2018). (Contra his second requirement, I later demonstrate that general obedience is not necessary for a legal system to exist.)

A threshold problem for Burazin's assertion is that legal systems are not unified entities in the sense conveyed by the notion of an artifact. A legal system is an abstraction encompassing congeries of courts, legislatures, prosecutor's offices, defender's offices, legal aid offices, police departments, police unions, public and private prisons, private lawyers and firms, law schools, bar associations, paralegals, case reports, law journals, and more (stenographers, clerks, etc.). The claim that all of the various activities, practices, organizations, and institutions comprising a legal system can be wrapped together as an intentionally created *entity* begs credulity. A courthouse is an organizational entity; a hierarchically organized judicial system is an entity encompassing the courts contained within it, but a legal system is a theoretical projection on many differentiated organizations that comprise complexes of heterarchical networks (Tamanaha 2021: chapter 4).

Artifact legal theorists might protest that my portrayal of "legal system" is too broad. Analytical jurisprudents commonly reduce law to a basic positivist account of legal officials following a shared set of rules for determining valid law within a territory (see Burazin 2016: 397–99; Ehrenberg 2016: 16–18; Roversi 2019: 53, 60). With respect to modern state legal systems, however, this account is too narrow. Since legal rules and enactments have meaning within a historically developed corpus of technical legal knowledge and concepts (Philips et al. 2004) and lawyers must be trained in this body of knowledge, jurists who develop and systematize legal knowledge and law professors who teach law must be included, although often they are not legal officials. In addition, private lawyers serve citizens and entities, although they are often not themselves legal officials. Without jurists, law professors, and private lawyers, the legal system is not functional, but adding these participants vastly multiplies and diversifies the intentions within legal systems.

The artifact account fails even if we focus only on legal officials because the specific intentions in their legal activities are oriented toward the *wrong object*. To repeat, for artifact theory, creators have in mind intentions about features and functions that determine the object they are making – with a direct *causal* connection between their intentions and the features of the object created. However, as described above, intentional states of legal actors are oriented toward and engaged in their immediate tasks. Legislators and judges work within *preexisting institutional structures* contemplating issues at hand based on the balance of considerations, engaging in routine legal actions. The propositional content of their intentions is not about creating the legal system, nor about the coordination function of law. This does not satisfy Burazin's stated requirement of a "particular intention" to create the legal system.

To answer this objection, artifact legal theorists might point to Searle's notion of collective intentionality, described previously. People engaging in collective actions characteristically have we-intentions oriented to the group activity. When participating in orchestras (a symphony) and football teams (a set play), each player carries out a designated role, knowing that their actions mesh with the roles played by other members, combining in a coordinated we-intended whole. Each person does not need to know in detail what the others are doing (although a quarterback and conductor must). "All one needs to believe is that they share one's collective goal and intend to do their part in achieving that goal" (Searle 2010: 45).

Legal systems are not like a football team or a specific play and not like an orchestra or a particular symphony. A crucial difference (among many) is that the actions of legal officials do not mesh together, and they do not share a collective goal of creating the legal system, whereas football teams have diagrammed plays and orchestras have symphony scores. Legal officials understand that their actions are connected in various ways: legislators know that the laws they enact are supposed to be enforced and applied by other legal officials; judges are supposed to apply the law enacted by the legislature; and the executive, prosecutors, police, and so on are supposed to carry out and enforce the law. Superficially, perhaps this resembles we-intention, except that this highly idealized picture masks the reality of disagreement and contestation within, among, and between these groups of legal officials at every level (federal, state, and municipal). Various legal officials have different roles, responsibilities, and agendas (including personal and ideological) that generate conflicts. Judges regularly interpret laws in ways different from what legislators intended; prosecutors and police regularly do not enforce legislation as written and sometimes defy or circumvent judicial orders; state and federal legal officials regularly clash; and so on. The often-mentioned gap between law in books and law in action recognizes that divergences are endemic (Pound 1910). Any football team or orchestra that operates in this fashion would fall apart. Perhaps the best evidence of shared intention is the oath of office that many legal officials swear to uphold the law and perform the duties of their office – but the goal reflected in this oath is a commitment to be bound by the law. A legal system – in the sense of tying together all official legal institutions in a unified whole – is a theoretical abstraction.

To surmount the difficulties in showing intentional creation, several artifact legal theorists either abandon intention or dilute it to the point of meaninglessness. Crowe (2014) and Burazin (2019a) encompass customary law by dropping intention and shifting to Searle's collective recognition (aside from we-intention) in the community; Roversi (2018: 95–96, 103–6, 2019: 51–2, 58) applies "the term 'intention-rooted' referring to a broad variety of phenomena, ranging from a specific creative intention to a simple regularity of behavior recognized afterwards as having constituted a legal institution" (Burazin 2019b: 233). Roversi writes, "their nature and content [legal institutions] may not be entirely transparent to us or immediately fixed by actual intentional states in the legal community" (2019: 52). These moves, however, are counter to the thrust of artifact theory that intentional creation causally determines the features/functions of the artifact. Stretching to account for law, they have de facto discarded artifact theory, sub silentio shifting to social constructionism, discussed in the next section.

As this critical engagement shows, the required connections between creators, intentions, objects, features, and functions in artifact theory are too narrow and demanding to meet for laws, legal institutions, and legal systems. The necessity for intentional creation, in particular, exhibits a systematic mismatch. There is a reason for this. Although Searle emphasized collective intentionality, he did not mean intentionality in the conscious sense. People operate within institutions that they take for granted, frequently acting in habitual routines, with their intentions not focused on the institutions themselves or on constitutive rules. As Searle observed, "They do not think of private property, and the institutions for allocating among private property, or human rights, or governments as human creations. They tend to think of them as part of the natural order of things, to be taken for granted in the same way they take for granted the weather or the force of gravity" (Searle 2010: 107). Individual actions occur within a pre-intentional, largely unself-conscious, socially infused backdrop: "the Background consists of the set of capabilities, dispositions, tendencies, practices, and so on that enable the intentionality to function, and the Network of intentionality consists of the set of beliefs, attitudes, desires, and so on to enable specific intentional states to function, that is, to determine their conditions of satisfaction" (2010: 155, 1995: 127–47). Searle thus offloaded a substantial part of intentionality to the Background of "nonintentional or preintentional capacities that enable intentional states of function" (Searle 1995: 129), which he identified with Wittgenstein on rule-following and sociologist Pierre Bourdieu's *habitus* (132). (Habitus is the notion that society is structured through systems of correlated schemes of perceptions, ideas, values, dispositions, and action that are incorporated, practiced, reinforced, and embodied within people (Marcoulatos 2003: 72–73).) Artifact legal theorists, however, omit this background.

By centering on intentionality, furthermore, artifact legal theory as well as Searle's collective intentionality cannot account for unintentional consequences or unintended emergent phenomena. Many social phenomena are not specifically collectively intended, though they are the product of intentional action. The division of labor in society formed as a result of innumerable individual decisions over time (Mead 2002: 106), though it was not intentionally created as such. People do not intentionally create "runs on banks" or business cycles. These are "non-intentional properties," but "they are both systemic and pervasive in social life and history" (Friedman 2006: 75). Unintentional aspects and consequences pervade law. Legal officials and lawyers do not intentionally create barriers to access to law, though it nonetheless exists in many societies owing to the high cost of legal services and limited resources of the poor. Police in the USA who detain, search, arrest, and kill black suspects in disproportionately high numbers do not intend to create a discriminatory criminal justice system, though it exists nonetheless. Systematic aspects of law exist that are not intentional, though they have features or functions (discussed later as latent functions).

Artifact legal theory obfuscates important aspects of law. Five problems with this theoretical frame stand out: First, presenting laws, legal institutions, and legal systems as *entities* (connoting a unified thing) conceptually obscures continuous clashes, disjunctions, disagreements, inconsistencies, variations, multiplicities, and changes within and among them. Second, object framing eliminates the processual aspects of law: enacting, applying, enforcing, and interpreting law are *processes* involving people doing law stuff within legal practices while influenced by surrounding factors (ideology, social pressure, etc.). Third, the focus on intentionally created features/functions of law analytically imposes a singular intention and function that often does not actually exist as such, while leaving out unintended aspects, functions, and consequences of law. Fourth, the intentional-creation-object focus of artifact theory does not pick up the socially encrusted sedimentation of law as a tradition interconnected within society with self-perpetuating, path-dependent features that enable, shape, and constrain legal actions and change, comprising the preexisting institutional contexts within which legal officials operate. Finally, construing law itself as an artifact distracts attention from the ways in which actual artifacts – offices, courtrooms, computers, files, memoranda, funding, and so forth – constitute the material dimensions of legal activities that help render them socially stable and enduring (Gorski 2016).

Artifact theory is a poor fit for law. This should not be surprising. A theory that holds that legislative acts, judicial decisions, property, legal systems, and so on are artifacts must squeeze complex, heterogeneous, contested, and ever-changing legal phenomena into the same theoretical box as shoes and chairs. Artifact legal theory produces no insights about law that cannot be obtained more immediately from social constructionism. In response to an objection along these lines, Roversi asserts, "An artifact theory of law does not claim to *replace* a socio-ontological, institutional theory of law, but rather proposes to *specify* such a theory, by stating that crucial to an understanding of the nature of law is the process by which abstract artifacts are constructed on the basis of collective recognition – a process through which legal institutions are hypostatized as abstract artifactual objects" (Roversi 2019: 59). But his response misses the point. Artifact theory is not an edifying specification. Social ontology and social constructionism address the entire social realm, of which artifacts are a subpart but not the whole. The stretching of artifact theory to include legal phenomena takes it outside the domain the theory is best suited to address while also distorting legal phenomena. This move is uncalled for because social ontology and social constructionism already naturally encompass legal institutions with no stretching of the theory or distortions of law.

3 Law as a Social Construction

The social world is the product of our meaningful actions and their intended and unintended consequences. Although it is constituted on an ongoing basis through these actions, it has an objective presence that preexists us and survives our passing. People are born into, assume a place in, partake of, and modify language, knowledge, conventions, social practices, institutions, and organiza-tions, collectively generated on an ongoing basis by the community of actors – giving rise to a common social world made up of hospitals, schools, petrol stations, banks, factories, government offices, courts, grocery stores, and every-thing else in society. These are the ubiquitous taken-for-granted socially con-structed phenomena within which we are daily immersed and engage in our projects.

Social construction is discussed across a wide range of matters, from the social construction of the sciences to postmodernism. Certain discussions focus on the social construction of ideas (beliefs, concepts, categories, theories, etc.), others on the social construction of "things" (objects, entities, organizations, institutions, etc.), and others consider both. The explanatory thrust of social constructionism involves recognition of the constitutive role of socially shared ideas and actions, along with contingency, historical development, and the possibility of change. Everything that exists in the social world can be con-structed differently through different ideas and actions. Many theorists who raise social constructionism challenge reification, emphasize contingency, pierce assumptions that things are fixed, and deny essential and necessary features (Diaz-Leon 2013). While natural phenomena exist ab initio, what we consider physical laws and facts are the product of socially constructed theoretical frameworks, and different frameworks can produce different facts, as shown by the differences between Newton's mechanistic theory of gravity and Einstein's general relativity, both valid and relied upon.

In "The Social Construction of the Concept of Law," Frederick Schauer expresses this cluster of ideas with respect to both the *concept of law* and *law as an institution*. He asserts "that not only are laws and entire legal systems humanly created, but also that law, far from being natural, is itself a human social construction" (Schauer 2005: 496). Accordingly, "it would be open for the people whose collective beliefs and actions construct (tautologically) that which is socially constructed – call it a 'society' or a 'culture' – to construct law in one way or another." The same holds for the changeability of the concept of law. Moreover, "different cultures might thus possess not only different legal institutions, but different concepts of law" (497), which vary and change over time.

Analytical jurisprudents widely accept that law is a social construction but seldom explicate what this entails beyond the obvious point that law is created through our actions. Its implications, I show, extend much further in ways that affect theories of law. For an account of the social construction of law, I build on a handful of concepts articulated by pragmatist philosopher and sociologist George Herbert Mead, incorporated in Berger and Luckmann's sociological classic, *The Social Construction of Reality* (1966), and in the work of Alfred Schutz, a pioneering social constructionist theorist. Mead's analysis is consistent with, though far more informative than, Searle's reductionist social ontology and does not rely on an artificially bracketed (obscure) Background. In the course of articulating Mead's position, I inject comments showing its implications for law.

Mead provided a naturalistic account of human social animals and characterized social institutions as emergent phenomena. Human thinking, he argued, is the product of symbolic social interaction through language and gestures, rendering the mind thoroughly social: "The internalization in our experience of the external conversations of gestures which we carry on with other individuals in the social process is the essence of thinking; and the gestures thus internalized are significant symbols because they have the same meanings for all individual members of the given society or social group" (Mead 1934: 47).

Two notions Mead articulated have been incorporated by contemporary scientific accounts of collective intentionality (Tomasello 2014: 122–23). The first is our ability to put ourselves in the position of the other, "taking the role of the other," which allows us to understand their role as well as see ourselves through the other's perspective (Mead 1934: 73, 109, 150). This creates a "reciprocity of perspectives" in social interaction, constituting a shared understanding that allows us to apprehend and anticipate one another's actions, expectations, and intentions (Schutz 1962: 11–13). The second notion is that humans internalize the perspective of a "generalized other" of the whole community (Mead 1934: 154). "A person who has in himself the universal response of the community toward that which he does, has in that sense the mind of the community" (268).

> The organized community or social group which gives to the individual his unity of self may be called the "generalized other." The attitude of the generalized other is the attitude of the whole community. Thus, for example, in the case of such a social group as a ball team, the team is the generalized other in so far as it enters – as an organized process or social activity – into the experience of any one of the individual members. (154)

This involves a shift from "many perspectives into something like 'any possible perspective,' which means, essentially, 'objective.' This 'any possible' or 'objective' perspective combines with a normative stance to encourage the inference that such things as social norms and institutional arrangements are objective parts of an external reality" (Tomasello 2014: 92). These conventions and institutional arrangements are historical inheritances of a given community. People who internalize the response of the community self-regulate as well as enforce conventional norms against others: "[T]he community exercises control over the conduct of its individual members; for it is in this form that the social process or community enters as a determining factor into the individual's thinking" (Mead 1934: 155). Extensive studies of childhood development confirm this process as integral to the development of children between the ages of three and six (Tomasello 2019).

With the first notion, humans understand the socially infused, intentional behavior of the people with whom they interact and see themselves reflectively from the standpoint of others; with the second notion, they share the community view and see themselves reflectively from the community as a whole, and they take the normative conventions and institutional structures of the community as objectively existing features of their world. Thus, while people think from the subjective first-person standpoint, human thinking is "collective, objective, reflective, and normative" (Mead 1934: 122–23). Individual minds are thus profoundly social. "The individual possesses a self only in relation to the selves of others members of his social group; and the structure of his self expresses or reflects the general behavior patterns of this social group to which he belongs, just as does the structure of the self of every other individual belonging to this social group" (164).

While portraying people with consummately social minds, Mead also emphasizes that people retain individuality. In addition to the generalized community, modern societies consist of many differentiated subgroups, including specialized ones with distinctive bodies of knowledge, concepts, modes of action, and practices (clubs, political parties, corporations, religious groups, physicists, sociologists, jurists, etc.; 157). People trained in law, for instance, operate in roles and practices of a particular legal system, internalizing legal knowledge and ways of thinking and doing law. At the same time, people occupy different positions in society, including positions in multiple social groups with various socially shared meanings, norms, and roles; a single person is a mother, judge, wife, churchgoer, club member, friend, and so on. People also have self-oriented as well as cooperative motivations and engage in projects to survive, achieve desired goods (including meaningful relationships and lives), and improve their material conditions. People have particular abilities, character traits, likes and dislikes, and the capacity for creativity and breaking away from conventions and norms. "Every individual self has its own individuality, its own unique pattern [and] does so from its own particular and unique standpoint within that process" (201).

A great deal of our social interaction occurs subconsciously through habits, conventions, and tactic knowledge. Reflective thought is brought to bear when we are confronted with problems, novel situations, confounded expectations, unexpected circumstances or events, confrontations that prompt alternative explanations and courses of action, anticipating likely consequences good and bad, and possible solutions. "The process of exercising intelligence is the process of delaying, organizing, and selecting a response or reaction to the stimuli of the given environmental situation" (100). Likewise, a great deal of legal actions, including lawyering and judging, occurs through habits, conventions, and tacit knowledge; reflective legal analysis occurs mainly in novel situations and when problems arise (see Dewey 1914).

Social institutions are interconnected within society and change over time. Mead observed, "The mere recitation of these essential social institutions [schools, churches, social control institutions, economic processes, means of communication] exhibits their vital relationship with one another . . . . No one institution could stand by itself, and the development of each one of them has been the outcome of the processes of all of them" (Mead 1938: 496). But society is "not an organic whole" (497). Social institutions and the people working within them or using them, while cooperating in many respects, also have clashing interests and competing demands for resources and power. "Each social institution with the good that it subtends asserts and maintains itself but finds itself in that assertion in conflict with other institutions and their goods" (498). Social institutions are stable but continuously change in relation to new developments (technology, economic booms and busts, natural disasters, etc.), competition for resources, critical reflections on current circumstances, problem-solving, and efforts to improve circumstances. Legal institutions are similarly interconnected with surrounding social institutions, and conflict and contestation among social institutions often take place on legal terrain as parties seek to control and wield law for particular objectives (Tamanaha 2006).

One implication of the temporal, historicist, changing dimensions of social existence is that the past enables and conditions the present while projecting toward the future; "that whatever emerges must be subject to the conditioning character of the present and that it must be possible to state the emergent in terms of the conditioning past" (Mead 2002: 86–87). Generally shared beliefs, existing institutional structures, and tools and technology embody accumulated social knowledge, composing a sedimentation of tradition – at the same time providing vehicles for future developments (Berger and Luckmann 1966: 67–72). Nothing emerges de novo or on a clean slate. "In the passage from the past into the future the present object is both the old and the new, and this holds for its relations to all other members of the system to which it belongs" (Mead 2002: 76–77). "Now, an extremely important fact is that the self-understandings which constitute social and psychological objects and events are inherently historical because they are subject to the constant change resulting from the various conceptual innovations [from internal and external sources] which a group's members introduce and come to accept" (Fay 1994: 100). Hence, legal concepts, doctrines, practices, and institutions are constituted and conditioned by their historical development within a legal tradition even as they continuously change.

Mead applied his views to law. He described the historical development of courts in naturalistic, evolutionary terms. What underlies criminal punishment as well as social solidarity, he observed, is a "hostile" instinct manifested in primitive impulses that reinforce group bonds and support compliance. "The revulsions against criminality reveal themselves in a sense of solidarity with the group, a sense of being a citizen on the one hand excludes those who have transgressed the laws of the group and on the other inhibits tendencies to criminal acts in the citizen himself" (Mead 1918: 586). Support for his speculations can be found in neurological studies, which show that when citizens administer punishments to norm violators parts of their brain linked to pain, anger, and disgust are activated (Wilson 2012: 250–51). "The decision to punish, the passionate motivation to do so, is a frothy limbic state"

(Sapolsky 2017: 610). Mead suggested that informal tribunals (presided by elders or chiefs) emerged to determine responsibility and sanctions to prevent tit-for-tat violence, the precursors of formal courts in highly differentiated modern societies.

He utilized "taking the role of the other" and the "generalized other" to help explain how property rights are socially constructed:

> The institution represents a common response on the part of all members of the community to a particular situation. This common response is one which, of course, varies with the character of the individual. In the case of theft the response of the sheriff is different from that of the attorney-general, from that of the judge and jurors, and so forth; and yet they all are responses which maintain property, which involve the recognition of property rights in others. There is a common response in varied forms. One appeals to the policeman for assistance, one expects the state's attorney to act, expects the court and its various functionaries to carry out the process of the trial of the criminal . . . . Such organized sets of responses are related to each other; if one calls out one such sets of responses, he is implicitly calling out others as well.
>
> Thus the institutions of society are organized forms of group or social activity – forms so organized that the individual members of society can act adequately and socially by taking the attitudes of others toward these activities. (Mead 1934: 261)

People within organizations (prosecutor's office, court, police department, etc.) are oriented toward particular purposes built on collectively recognized roles, responsibilities, routines, practices, and rules, engaging in activities with various connections to what others are doing in other legal institutions. Under this account, neither the community nor legal officials intentionally create the legal system as such. Instead, legal organizations gradually evolved historically subject to surrounding influences into existing institutional arrangements, which in the aggregate – in the generalized other from any possible perspectives – comprise the legal system.

Organizational structures are constructed through rules and roles revolving around purposive activities, typically supported by a material base consisting of buildings, tools (computers, etc.), record keeping, financial resources, and so on. People within organizations are immersed in common practices that combine conventions, knowledge, normative orientations, and standards of conduct – the clusters of characteristic ways of doing those activities. Judges, for example, use and are influenced by legal knowledge, legal reasoning, and the norms of the judicial role and felt obligations to other judges and litigants when engaging in judging; police use skills in observation and investigation, duties to the public, obligations to fellow officers, and so on when engaging in policing;

and so forth. People partake of, are influenced by, and perpetuate these complexes of practices, bodies of knowledge, and institutions, which amount to subcultures and ways of life.

Mead also stressed, however, that people's actions *are not strictly determined* by their institutional roles and responsibilities and a pluralism of perspectives exists owing to differences among individuals and social groups. Practices, roles, and norms afford "plenty of scope for originality, flexibility, and a variety of such conduct" (Mead 1934: 262). This is why judges on appellate panels can sincerely disagree about the interpretation of legal provisions, often along ideological alignments, and write reasoned legal justifications for opposing outcomes.

Mead combined holism, historicism, and conflict to explain changes in socially constructed conceptions of legal rights over time. His historical analysis shows that each formulation of rights – by Hobbes, by Locke, in the Declaration of Independence, in the French Declaration of the Rights of Man, and so on – was made with specific "dangers and hindrances" and particular objectives in mind (Mead 1915: 142). Thereafter, the rights become abstract, deprived of their original meaning, whereupon further contexts of application arise that produce new meanings. "We started with life, liberty, security, equality, pursuit of happiness, as natural rights," Mead observed, but they were "incapable of definition as to their content" (150). As social, political, and economic views change and new clashes between interests arise, the meanings of rights are filled in differently. "It is evident that categories which are to serve all these purposes must be abstract and empty of content and that they should get their content through the struggle which arises on the bare floor and between their distant walls" (151). The searing contest of his day was between laborers and employers, playing out in legislatures and courts as a clash between social welfare and labor legislation versus liberty of contract and property rights enforced by courts (152).

Mead's account of rights shows how law is infused with meaning through ongoing social contestation, conveying that law is not just a reflection of social and moral norms but also a site of continuous struggle between individual and social interests seeking to enlist and wield the law to serve their interests and goals. His dynamic depiction starkly contrasts with accounts by analytical jurisprudents that law consists of a system of rules that maintain social order (taken up later).

4 Five Implications of Social Constructionism

Social constructionism, particularly Mead's account, opens a host of potential insights for legal theory, ranging from the process of and influences on judicial decision-making, legal variation and change, how law constitutes aspects of society and in turn is shaped by social forces, how law is constructed through individual and collective projections of law, and more. Five points of direct relevance to contemporary analytical jurisprudence will be summarily stated here (several elaborated in later sections).

First, social constructionism suffers none of the puzzles and limitations of artifact legal theory while offering fuller, more adequate insights into legal phenomena. Laws, legal institutions, legal organizations, and legal systems are not singular entities intentionally created by authors or creators but involve manifold, continuous social and historical processes, which arise and evolve through complicated interactions (and reactions) of social interests, contestation, and individual actions, with intentional and unintentional consequences. Rather than positing creators intentionally creating laws, legal institutions, and legal systems, it posits a preexisting social legal world formed through the aggregate actions of preceding generations and contemporaries that legal actors and members of the community come into, internalize, participate in, perpetuate, challenge, modify, and develop.

The second point is that social constructionism incorporates naturalistic causation. Mead was influenced by evolutionary theory and placed human social interaction on a continuum with animals generally. Social construction itself is naturally generated and constrained, part of the natural world, shaped by natural human traits and social requirements. Consequently, it does not follow from social constructionism, as Schauer observed, that "law is not natural in any interesting way" (Schauer 2005: 496). On the contrary, socially constructed law has deep naturalistic connections. If law is a product of the natural aspects of human social ordering, a basic corpus of such laws should exist within communities, and other patterns in connection with law and social requirements will exist, though exhibiting a great deal of variation and change.

The third implication challenges a basic aspect of the methodological stance of contemporary legal philosophers. When legal philosophers contemplate the nature of law, they abstract law from surrounding conditions and forces, whereas social constructionism views law as inextricably intertwined with and interacting with other social institutions, sees multiple manifestations of law (explained next), and pays attention to variations and change in law and in law's role within society across varying social contexts and over time. This entails a shift from isolating on law statically conceived to a dynamic, diachronic and synchronic view of law.

The fourth point is that the collective recognition aspect of social constructionism shifts to a ground-up perspective on law, generating insights overlooked by legal theorists who analyze law through intuitions based on the concept of state law, a top-down projection. *The* crucial factor in the social construction of all social institutions, including law, is collective recognition within a given group. Collective recognition determines *who* counts as legal officials; *which* specified legal powers they exercise – as legislators, judges, prosecutors, police, and so on; *when* (the circumstances in which) their actions count as legal; and *what* qualifies as law. Based on a projected top-down image of state law, analytical jurisprudents almost uniformly analyze law in terms of two conjoined elements: a legal system run by officials and the territorial society it addresses – what I call the monist law state. Social constructionism, in contrast, starts with communities that collectively recognize law (thereby constituting it), which exposes that in many societies more than one form of law is recognized, a reality long neglected by legal philosophers.

The fifth point, following from the preceding, bears on the classic question "What is law?" The singular – *is* – formulation of the question assumes that law takes a single form composed of set features. However, if collectively recognized law has evolved along with social changes, it is conceivable that law has assumed different forms and functions across societies and over time. Hence, although commonalities may exist tied to natural human traits and requirements of social life, manifestations of law do not necessarily possess essential and necessary features.

In closing, I mention one implication that *does not* necessarily follow from social construction: that social constructions cannot be natural kinds. "I believe that law is a social construction and not a natural kind," Schauer stated, implying that they are mutually exclusive (Schauer 2005: 496). If, for naturalistic reasons, law with certain shared features independently emerge in human communities or are copied to meet the same needs, an argument can be made that certain manifestations of law are types of natural kinds (albeit with clusters of features) (see Khalid 2019; Millikin 1999). Humans are by nature social animals, and in this sense, human social creations are continuous with natural products. In other work, I have inductively grouped conventionally recognized forms of law into three categories with characteristic features – fundamental laws of social intercourse, regime law, and cross-polity law – which perhaps point in this direction (Tamanaha 2021). Assertions of this sort must be established analytically and be backed with compelling empirical evidence, which does not yet exist, though the possibility cannot be ruled out.

With the preceding overview of social constructionism in mind, I now examine a series of central claims about law proffered by analytical jurisprudents.

5 Idealized Accounts of the Functions of Law

Many legal philosophers present social functions as a fundamental aspect of law (see Moore 1992: 213). Epitomizing this sentiment, Joseph Raz observed that "all legal systems *necessarily* perform, at least to a minimal degree, which I am unable to specify, social functions of all types to be mentioned [guiding behavior, settling disputes, providing services, etc.], and that these are all the main types of social functions that they perform" (Raz 2009b: 167, emphasis added). Theories that center on law's functions can be placed in one of three categories. The most ambitious claim is that law is a functional kind. A second strong claim is law's function explains the existence of law, although it is not necessary or sufficient to the nature of law (Ehrenberg 2016). Third, many legal theorists identify the functions of law as guiding conduct or coordinating behavior or maintaining social order by quelling disruptions and resolving disputes – though they do not necessarily claim that law exists owing to these functions. There are multiple theories in each category, and the issues they raise are too involved to detail (for a critique, see Green 1998). In this section, I apply a sociological perspective to critically examine the first two categories, taking up the third category in Section 7.

First, a few words must be said about functions. The function is usually understood in teleological terms: the purpose or end something serves. This purpose may be intentionally conferred by a designer (this is artifact theory), or it may be selected through evolutionary processes without a designer (i.e., the function of a heart is to circulate blood). Analytical jurisprudents making strong functional claims place great weight on a distinction between a "mere" function and "proper" function. A mere function involves what role something plays, what it tends to do, and how it functions. A proper function, in contrast, is what that thing is for, the end that explains its existence. "A mere function or capacity is anything an object does or is capable of doing. A proper function, on the other hand, is not just any capacity or effect which an object has, or even the common tendencies and patterns of use and effects which an object is prone to display – it is a capacity or effect which an object has which it is, in some sense, *supposed* to have *by virtue of being that kind of object*. It explains why it is the (kind of) object it is. It is the essential aim of the object" (Mihal 2017: 126). What determines the aim it is supposed to have is that it has been designed or selected for that purpose. Ehrenberg summarizes, "A thing's proper function is the characteristic ends that it yields (or is supposed to yield) which explain its presence, development, or selection" (Ehrenberg 2016: 21). The proper function entails the normative element that the thing selected is *good for* serving that function, though it does not require that it always serve it (failure is possible). Nor does it require that it only serve that function.

Significantly, certain analytical jurisprudents have utilized this distinction to dismiss unintended or latent functions of law as not proper functions (as Ehrenberg holds). The manifest-latent distinction was articulated by sociologist Robert Merton: "manifest functions" are "those objective consequences contributing to the adjustment or adaptation of the system which are intended and recognized by participants in the system"; "latent functions" are objective consequences "which are neither intended nor recognized" by the participants (Merton 1957: 51). For the Hopi rain dance, for instance, the manifest (intended) function is to bring rain to the planting, while the latent function is to enhance group solidarity (unintended consequence). The challenge for unintentional functionalist explanation is the logical impermissibility of explaining a cause through its subsequent effects. Enhancing group solidarity cannot cause the dance that enhances group solidarity. Rather, the dance must arise for a *current* disposition it satisfies – like a natural human propensity for collective rhythmic movement and the immediate pleasure it brings to participants and observers – while having the effect of enhancing social solidarity in a way that contributes to the persistence of the dance and the collectivity. Ignoring latent functions provides a distorted view of law, I will show.

Legal philosopher Michael Moore insightfully examines law in functional terms (Moore 1992: 212–17). A condensed version of his analysis suffices for the purposes here. To get the analysis off the ground, Moore explains, a theorist must posit what law is. Then one formulates a provisional list of law's features, for example, coercive sanctions and habits of obedience (Austin), regulation of its own creation (Kelsen), the union of primary and secondary rules (Hart), moral authority (Finnis), and so on. Then one identifies the end or function of law: subject human conduct to the guidance of rules (Fuller), enhance autonomy and liberty through legal predictability (Hayek), enhance group survival (Hart), promote the common good (Finnis), and so on. A theorist then examines the connections between the features and functions she identifies, starting from the features to determine if they are necessary means to the end, as well as starting with the end to determine the structure it entails. As this analysis reflects, theories of law typically consist of a combination of form and function (Tamanaha 2017: chapter two; more on this later).

A "serious objection" Moore considers is "that it just assumes that law serves a goal (that is, that law is a functional kind)" (Moore 1992: 219). The analysis is "question-begging" because asking about the end of law assumes that law *has* an end. The answer of proponents of functional views of law is that law has been designed or selected for this end. This response, however, merely pushes the inquiry back to whether law is indeed a designed or selected artifact for particular ends. If the better account is that law is an institutionalized system for declaring and enforcing laws backed by coercion that is utilized in many ways for a multitude of purposes, then it is an instrument with no particular or characteristic end (Green 1998; Tamanaha 2017). Legal systems, then, serve as an institutionalized means.

To delve deeper into doubts about functional claims, we must unpack a two-part assumption that undergirds functional analyses of law: law has (1) "characteristic ends" (function) that (2) serves society as a whole (the broader social unit served by function). These assumptions are based on the image of the monist law state elaborated later. The first assumption is problematic because law does many things – so what identifies certain things but not others as *characteristic* of law? Consider that all state legal systems have laws that serve government power and the legal system itself: taxes, fees, customs; laws against sedition, insurrection, and treason; law requiring mandatory service (military, jury, etc.); laws prohibiting lying to or resisting officials; and more. But no functionalist analysis identifies the ends of law as serving the power of government and the law itself, though this is a characteristic feature of state law.

Surely, the government and legal system do not exist for their own sake, most legal theorists would insist, but rather to serve society, so the ultimate purpose of laws that serve government power is to enable it to serve social ends. Implicitly relying on this assumption, many legal philosophers have articulated idealized accounts of law's purported functions for society. However, many authoritarian regimes past and present have existed and utilized law primarily to maintain their grip on power (see North Korea today). Adam Smith observed, "A government is often maintained, not for the nation's preservation, but its own" (Smith 1982: 547).

This brings us to the second assumption – that law serves society as a whole. Anthropology, archaeology, and history tell a less benign story about law. Societies larger than hunter-gatherers – chiefdoms and early states that separately emerged in various locations around the world – exhibit a consistent pattern of legally enforced inequality (see Flannery and Marcus 2012). A leading scholar of state development, Henri Claessen, remarked, "there is *always* found great inequality in (early) states. Some people, the happy few, are rich and powerful and all others, the great majority, are poor and powerless" (Claessen 2002: 104, emphasis added). Law maintained this arrangement. "One of the most dramatic innovations of states is that the central government monopolizes the use of force, dispensing justice according to the rules of law" (Flannery and Marcus 2012: 476). Hammurabi's Code is replete with status distinctions that enforce the power of the elite and men over women, children, lower classes, and slaves. Under Roman law, everyone beneath the freeborn male Roman citizen (women, children, and slaves) suffered varying degrees of legal restrictions. From the sixteenth through the twentieth centuries, Western colonial legal regimes across Africa, Asia, and the Pacific subjugated indigenous populations to serve the political and economic interests of colonial powers and their settler populations. Slavery and Jim Crow laws in the United States held African Americans in legally imposed bondage and degradation to whites.

Theorists extending back centuries have declared that law serves the powerful at the expense of others in society. Rudolph von Jhering wrote, "Whoever will trace the legal fabric of a people to its ultimate origins will reach innumerable cases where the force of the stronger has laid down the law for the weaker" (Jhering 1914: 185). Adam Smith trenchantly observed: "Laws and government may be considered in this and indeed in every case as a combination of the rich to oppress the poor, and preserve to themselves the inequality of the goods which would otherwise soon be destroyed by the attacks of the poor, who if not hindered by the government would soon reduce the others to an equality with themselves by open violence" (Smith 1982: 208). This view of law goes back millennia, voiced in Plato's *Republic* by Thrasymachus:

> And the different forms of government make laws democratical, aristocratical, tyrannical, with a view to their several interests; and these laws, which are made by them for their own interests, are the justice which they deliver to their subjects, and him who transgresses them they punish as a breaker of the law, and unjust. And that is what I mean when I say that in all states there is the same principle of justice, which is the interest of the government; and as the government must be supposed to have power, the only reasonable conclusion is, that everywhere there is one principle of justice, which is the interest of the stronger. (Plato 1991: 20)

Oliver Wendell Holmes matter-of-factly opined, "whatever body may possess the supreme power for the moment is certain to have interests inconsistent with others which have competed unsuccessfully. The more powerful interests must be more or less reflected in legislation" (Holmes 1873: 583). H. L. A. Hart came close to asserting that this reflects human nature when he observed, "So long as human beings can gain sufficient co-operation from some to enable them to dominate others, they will use the forms of law as one of their instruments" (Hart 1994: 210).

Abundant historical evidence supports the assertion that among the characteristic functions of law is structuring and enforcing the domination of certain interests in society over others. Functionalist theories propounded by analytical jurisprudents, however, rarely declare the domination function of law. Why omit the ubiquity of legal domination? Legal philosophers do not see themselves as purposefully concealing its untoward elements, yet their idealized functionalist accounts of law have that effect. Epitomizing this stance, Scott Shapiro declares, "the *fundamental aim* of the law is to rectify the moral deficiencies associated with the circumstances of legality"; "law's *mission* is to address the moral defects of alternative forms of social ordering" (Shapiro 2011: 213, emphasis added).

Functional analysis by analytical jurisprudence is constricted by two blinders that produce a sanitized account of the functions of law. One blinder, already mentioned, is the assumption that law serves the *society or community as a whole*, rather than a subpart thereof or the government itself (and the social groups that control and benefit from the government). The second blinder inheres in the theoretical move to count only "proper" functions. Proper functions, to repeat, are those functions that are intentionally designed or that are designed or selected.

When law is used for domination, often it is *not intentional domination*. Law is seen as good and right or the natural order of things through ideological, religious, traditional, or cultural justifications, which constitute shared beliefs about law. Even those who are dominated might not recognize it as such, viewing their condition as appropriate or natural. Millennia ago, "Laws were often claimed to originate with the Gods, who transmitted them to humans through the proclamations of rulers" (Trigger 2003: 221). "The Babylonian king Hammurabi claimed to have assembled his law code at the command of the god Utu, or Shamas, who, because as the sun god he saw everything that humans did, was also the patron deity of justice" (222).

This applies to modern societies as well. In the United States, well into the twentieth century, women could not vote; property was in the name of husbands; legal claims related to a wife were the claims of the husband; and a husband could not be charged with raping his wife, among other legal disadvantages. This was not intentional legal domination of men over women but involved long-standing legal rules that reflected cultural and religious beliefs about women and marriage. In an 1876 ruling that upheld the prohibition of women from practicing law, the United State Supreme Court cited "the law of the Creator" that the "paramount destiny and mission of women are to fulfill the noble and benign offices of wife and mother" (*Bradwell* v. *Illinois* 1876: 142). Many legal systems throughout history and today have imposed systematic legal disabilities on women, not because men intentionally design the law to subjugate women but because under prevailing beliefs the laws are believed to be right. Yet women are nonetheless legally subjugated.

As this analysis shows, the limitation to "proper" functions eliminates a huge swath of what law does. Furthermore, this discussion reinforces the previous point that by fastening on *intentions*, artifact theories, functionalist theories, and Searle's collective intentionality are flawed because they leave out social elements that enable, shape, and constrain intentional actions (Searle placed this in the Background). People have socially infused minds and shared meaning and operate within preexisting socially generated ideational and institutional contexts – composed of and surrounded by interconnected cultural, customary, moral, legal, economic, technological, and ecological factors – which they do not intentionally create as such. Theories that build exclusively on intentions are deficient because a good deal of what matters in the socially constructed world, including law, are pre-given, pre-conscious, pre-intentional ideas, beliefs, structures, practices, and institutions.

The most ambitious functional account treats law as a *functional kind* – the claim that the nature of law is captured by its function. All such arguments inevitably fail owing to two aspects of the relationship between things and functions: *multiple utilizability* and *functional equivalents*. First, most things can be utilized in multiple ways to serve multiple functions. Law cannot be identified in terms of a single function because law does multiple things. A formulation sufficiently general to encompass all possible uses – for example, law's function is to effectuate systems of rules; the function of law is to serve as a means – is uninformative. Second, most functions can be served in more than one way. If the nature of something is defined in terms of its function, everything that serves the same function is encompassed. Consequently, when law is defined in terms of coordinating behavior or maintaining social order, anything that coordinates behavior or maintains order *is* law, which results in over-inclusiveness. For these reasons, Ehrenberg recognizes that functions cannot provide the basis for necessary and sufficient features of law, instead taking the less demanding position that "any adequate explanation of law must do so in terms of the social function it performs" (though he excludes latent functions because they are not intentional) (Ehrenberg 2016: 46).

A recent argument by Jan Mihal that law is a functional kind results in over-inclusiveness. He posits that the function of law is to guide conduct and maintain social order. He accepts that language, customs, morals, habits, etiquette, and other social phenomena also maintain social order – they are functional equivalents of law. Mihal invokes "proper" functions to screen out these other modes of social ordering, asserting, "while moral norms, habits, and social customs might happen to maintain social order, it is not nearly as plausible that they are selected for or designed because they maintain social order" (Mihal 2017: 131). This assertion, for which he offers no explanation or empirical support, is offered ad hoc – yet another idealization that renders law special, the chosen one (literally). Andrei Marmor observes, "Law is not the only normative domain in our culture; morality, religion, social conventions, etiquette, and so on, also guide human conduct in many ways which are similar to law" (Marmor 2019). Given the closeness of law with moral norms and customs (think of customary law) and their substantial functional overlap, it is dubious to suggest that law alone was designed or selected for the same function, while the others were not, nor can this question be resolved through philosophical speculation, since design or selection is an empirical causal claim. Mihal ultimately acknowledges that these other social phenomena might have been designed and selected to maintain social order: "In this case, they would have to be considered members of the functional kind 'law' since they have the same proper function" (132). As a consequence, morals, customs, habits, and so on *are* law. This result is compelled by the logic of functional analysis. In Section 9, I explain why all attempts to define law in terms of form and function are stymied by this problem.

6 The Dis-Embeddedness of Legal Systems from Lived Social Relations

An assumption nigh universally held among analytical jurisprudents is that law guides social behavior. This assumption will be critically examined in the next section. To set up that discussion, first, I must highlight an essential implication of legal systems that has received scant attention. The guidance function of law plays a determinative role in Hart's fable of the emergence of law to solve the problem of uncertainty in (prelegal) primitive societies. In societies governed by regimes of primary rules alone (by customary law), he tells us, uncertainty prevails when doubts exist about what the rules are or their scope of application. "The simplest form of remedy for the *uncertainty* of the regime of primary rules is the introduction of what we shall call a rule of 'recognition.' This will specify some feature or features possession of which by a suggested rule is taken as a conclusive affirmative indication that it is a rule of the group to be supported by the social pressure it exerts," he wrote (Hart 1994: 92). The conventionally recognized rule of recognition provides the basis for secondary rules – the body of rules legal officials utilize to recognize, change, and apply the primary rules that are obligatory for the social group.

Importantly, Hart warns about a danger that comes with the emergence of institutions manned by legal officials to create a legal system:

> [T]he step from the simple form of society, where primary rules of obligation are the only means of social control, into the legal world with its centrally

organized legislature, courts, officials, and sanctions brings its solid gains at a certain cost. The gains are those of adaptability to change, certainty, and efficiency, and these are immense; the cost is the risk that the centrally organized power may well be used for the oppression of numbers with whose support it can dispense, in a way that the simpler regime of primary rules could not. (Hart 1994: 202)

This is a timeless concern (Green 2008; Waldron 1999). It reinforces the point pressed earlier that the weight of empirical evidence indicates that a characteristic function of law is to enforce domination by the government itself and by certain groups in society over others.

Hart accorded less attention, however, to a separate set of consequences with deleterious implications for legal certainty and the guidance function of law – consequences that operate contrary to the thrust of his claims. Legal systems by their very existence give rise to a number of uncertainties. To put it in strong terms, the creation of legal systems staffed by officials gives rise to an ontological gap between rules declared and enforced by legal officials and rules actually followed in social life. An ontological gap is created because their respective conditions of existence differ. For a legal system to exist, at the very least the *legal officials* must collectively recognize and utilize the rules of the system itself (primary and secondary). In contrast, customary law exists when the legal rules are widely accepted as standards within the community and reflected in social behavior. Uncertainty for the community is produced by legal systems because there is no guarantee that what legal officials recognize and enforce as law comports with what people in the community recognize as law.

Legal systems staffed by legal officials in effect *dis-embed* law from the community (see Postema 2008). The point merits emphasis: a uniquely legal system–generated uncertainty exists about whether what officials recognize as law is congruent with what the community believes is law – an uncertainty that does not exist in the absence of an institutionalized legal system manned by legal officials. An additional type of uncertainty exists owing to the capacity of legal officials to declare and change law by their will, at any moment, which cannot suddenly occur with rules of customary law followed by the community. Yet another uncertainty arises from specialized legal knowledge, procedures, and practices utilized by legal officials in their legal activities, and efforts by jurists to systematize and rationalize law, which creates legal concepts and reasoning laypeople may not apprehend. In modern societies, this dis-embeddedness from the community, and resultant uncertainties, has been exacerbated by the immense volume of laws produced by legal officials and the highly technical terminology, concepts, and processes they utilize.

To say legal systems are dis-embedded emphatically does not mean they are autonomous; law is integrated within and pervasively subject to social influences. What it means, put simply, is that a group of legal officials have the power to declare what counts as law, which creates the possibility that what they enact and enforce as law has no necessary connection with prevailing social norms and understandings.

The dis-embeddedness of legal systems from the community through institutional differentiation and the uncertainties it creates exists even when legal officials claim to recognize the customs and moral norms of the community. Jeremy Bentham marked the distinction between the customs of judges (custom "*in foro*") from the customs followed in society (custom "*in pays*") (Bentham 1977: 165–80). Eugen Ehrlich drew a similar distinction between "norms for decision" and "legal propositions" utilized by courts and jurists versus "rules of conduct" within social associations ("living law") (Ehrlich 1936: 121–36). Studies of African customary law distinguish between "juridical customary law" recognized by courts and "living customary law" followed in the community (Woodman 2011: 24–25, 27). In his magisterial survey of Western legal thought, Donald Kelley observes that this detachment is a common consequence of legal systems: "even with the provisio of popular 'approval' and 'tacit consent,' custom lost its primary ties with its social base and came under the control of legal and political authorities"; "the true significance of the transition from 'custom' to 'customary law' ... is that once again the legal experts have taken over" (Kelley 1990: 106).

Hart claimed that a benefit of legal systems is to reduce uncertainty among the populace about applicable legal norms. As this discussion reveals, however, legal systems create significant countervailing uncertainties through the ontological separation between norms followed within the community and norms recognized by the legal system, with significant implications largely overlooked by analytical jurisprudents.

7 The Purported Guidance Function of Law

The notion that the function of law is to guide conduct has a central place in legal philosophy. It coincides with the coordination function, mentioned earlier, in that people are able to coordinate their activities through the guidance provided by law. In an often-cited passage, H. L. A. Hart remarked, "I think it is quite vain to seek any more specific purpose which law as such serves beyond providing guides to human conduct and standards of criticism of such conduct" (Hart 1994: 249). Joseph Raz connects his exclusive legal positivist theory of law's claim to authority to the social sources thesis and guidance function of law in three steps: (1) law presents itself as a binding authority without regard to any other justification; (2) "It does so and can only do so by providing publicly ascertainable ways of guiding behavior and regulating aspects of social life"; and (3) "it follows that it must be possible to identify those [binding legal] rulings without engaging in a justificatory argument," so law must be identifiable exclusively in terms of social sources (Raz 2009b: 51–52). "Legal systems . . . do provide guidance to individuals. They contain laws determining the rights and duties of individuals. These are laws which courts are bound to apply in settling disputes and it is because of this that they also provide an indication to individual as to their rights and duties in litigation before the court," Raz explains (112). Moreover, "it is the essence of law that it expects people to be aware of its existence and, when appropriate, to be guided by it" (95). Along similar lines, Scott Shapiro argues that inclusive legal positivism is false because the incorporation of moral standards as law cannot satisfy the guidance function of law (Shapiro 2000). "We can say that the function of the legal rules is to guide conduct because they have been produced by legal institutions in order to guide conduct," he writes (169). Gerald Postema identifies guidance as *the* characteristic way law operates: "The core *modus operandi* of law is to guide the actions of intelligent, self-directing agents by addressing to them general norms to which their actions are expected to conform" (Postema 2008: 50).

The previous passages tie the guidance function of law to efficacy in three respects. First, the rule of recognition must be efficacious, that is, it must be conventionally observed by legal officials to identify what counts as valid law. In the absence of efficacy among legal officials, the legal system would not exist or function to create law. Second, assuming laws are declared through conventionally followed rules of recognition, legal officials must actually carry out (execute and apply) the law. In the absence of this efficacy, law would not actually guide the behavior of legal officials and consequently would not guide the behavior of the populace. Third, the subject populace must actually be guided by and generally obey the law. Discussion of general public obedience to law is deferred to the next section (the social efficacy thesis). Here, I critically examine the often-asserted guidance function of law.

First, we must know what guidance means. At a minimum, to be guided by a law requires that an agent knows the content of the law and conforms to what the law specifies ("epistemic guidance"); this can include (though does not require) that the agent be motivated to conform solely because of the rule ("motivational guidance") (Shapiro 2000: 146). As Shapiro put it, "if a rule is to have the function of guiding conduct, then the action that it is supposed to bring about is one in which the rule secures conformity by making a difference to the practical reasoning of an agent" (167). Two distinct audiences are guided: the rules guide the actions of legal officials when enforcing and applying the law and guide the conduct of people in the community subject to the law.

While the notion that law guides the conduct of the populace is nigh taken for granted among analytical jurisprudents, there is an obvious reason to doubt it, articulated by Andrei Marmor: "[P]eople can only be guided by rules or prescriptions if they know about the existence of the rule or prescription," yet "most people do not know the vast majority of laws of their country" (Marmor 2004: 5, 16). People generally know that they cannot rob, assault, and kill others (which most people don't want to do anyway) and pay their taxes and follow traffic laws, but beyond a general sense of a few matters, people know little about law and do not routinely think about the law as they go about their daily affairs. An incalculably vast number of civil, criminal, and regulatory statutes and common law provisions exist in the USA at federal, state, county, and municipal levels. Although the total number of criminal statutes in the USA is unknown, one estimate is that as many as 4,500 federal crimes exist, with dozens of new criminal statutes added each year, on top of thousands of state and municipal crimes, along with an untold number of federal, state, and municipal regulatory provisions with criminal and civil penalties (Cottone 2015: 141–42). The overwhelming proportion of civil, criminal, and regulatory provisions are not common knowledge among the populace.

Analytical jurisprudents must explain how law guides social conduct given the lack of knowledge about law, particularly since guidance requires that "the rule secures conformity by *making a difference to the practical reasoning of an agent*" (Shapiro 2000: 167). The objection that people do not know the law is "beside the point," Marmor answers, because most laws don't affect people in their daily lives and they can consult lawyers when a need arises (Marmor 2004:16). Shapiro asserts, "There are many ways an agent can learn about the law. He can read legal how-to-books, speak to criminals, consult lawyers, and so on" (Shapiro 2000: 150). These are remarkably cavalier responses to a direct challenge to a fundamental claim about law. They assume that people would know how to find law and comprehend the legal how-to book or have the financial wherewithal to consult lawyers. But studies have found high levels of unmet legal needs, with people foregoing lawyers in civil and criminal cases because they lack sufficient resources (Hadfield and Heine 2016).

If the vast majority of people do not consult lawyers *prior to* engaging in actions governed by legal rules, then they are not actually guided by officially declared law – it does not factor into their practical reasoning. Instead, to the extent that people think about law at all, they are guided by their *assumptions* about the law. And therein lies the rub: dozens of empirical studies extending back decades (most conducted in the United States and the UK) show that people have *incorrect* beliefs about law a significant percentage of time on matters directly relevant to their lives, including employment law, criminal law, family law, housing law, and consumer law (see Rowell 2019; van Rooij 2020). Erroneous beliefs about law have also been found among professionals like educators and doctors on matters relating to their work. People tend to think the law *is* what they believe the law *should* be (Darley et al. 2001; Kim 1999; Rowell 2019). In the USA, for example, many people believe that certain legal protections restrict employers' ability to fire employees, which do not actually exist (Kim 1999).

Contrary to repeated assertions by analytical jurisprudents about the guidance function of law, at least with respect to the behavior of most people most of the time (aside from companies and wealthy people who use lawyers to engage in transactions), law often functions ex post, after the behavior occurs, rather than ex ante (van Rooij 2020). Consulting law ex post cannot guide behavior. The divergence between views of law held by the public and laws issued by legal officials – an indication that law is regularly out of sync with normative views within the community – is a manifestation of the dis-embeddedness of law described in the preceding section.

The only serious philosophical effort to grapple with these issues is Gerald Postema's account of how law *indirectly* guides behavior. Postema recognizes that "merely coincidental correlations of behavior with standing legal norms fail to manifest law's effectiveness. To do so, it must be possible to attribute the behavior to law's efforts and operation, traced to properties or powers of law. Moreover, since effectiveness is said to be essential for the existence of law, these properties or powers must be part of the nature of law" (Postema 2008: 50). Yet, he acknowledges, rarely do citizens have more than a rudimentary grasp of the law; they have limited access to legal material; and they lack the capacity to understand legal norms (52–53). How, then, can law factor into practical reasoning?

Postema's answer builds on what he identifies as three features of law. First, general legal rules address, not just individuals, but members of the public "engaged in thick networks of interdependent social interaction" (54). Second, law does not involve individual rules in isolation, but rather "law addresses law-subjects as a system, and the normative guidance it offers takes the form of providing a framework of practical reasoning rather than that of a discrete general command" (55). Third, law involves three modes of guidance: a *directive* mode (prescribing classes of action), an *evaluative* mode (providing standards for evaluating behavior), and a *constitutive* mode (constituting relations between employers/employees, lessors/lessees, spouses, etc.; 55). In the constitutive mode, law operates "not as an explicit premise for deliberation, but as the context within which deliberation takes place and from which the elements prominently figuring in it have their practical significance" (55). Law provides effective guidance *indirectly*, Postema argues, through shaping and giving shape to "the network of informal social customs, conventions, and practices that structure the daily lives of those governed by law" (56).

In his account, law's guidance operates via the *mediation* of social customs, practices, and conventions. This relationship requires a close congruence or fit between law and society: "The *congruence thesis* holds that a substantial degree of congruence between the modes of reasoning of a legal system and the informal social customs, practices, and modes of reasoning that predominate in the society governed by it is a necessary condition of the existence of that legal system" (56–57). (Later, I show that the necessity claim is incorrect.) This necessity, Postema observes, is a driving force within law: "Because congruence is necessary for law's efficacy, law must seek to guide conduct through assimilating and transforming social practices and in doing so make itself vulnerable to being tailored to fit the dimensions of social practice" (61). He asserts, in other words, that *legal officials* are compelled by necessity to seek a close fit between legal norms and social practices.

Though his account is an illuminating effort to situate law in social surroundings, it is not fully consistent with the empirical evidence. Postema's theory is arguably able to explain how law indirectly guides behavior even when people *do not know the law*. But the explanation does not work in light of studies that consistently show that people often have an *incorrect understanding of the law* on common matters – with error rates exceeding 50 percent on certain matters. Whether directly or indirectly, law cannot guide behavior when people hold erroneous beliefs about what the law requires. Substantial error rates indicate that the extent to which law is shaped by, and shapes, prevailing social customs, conventions, and practices falls short of the "substantial degree of congruence" Postema requires as a necessary condition of law. Sources of information about law for members of the public include television shows, news, online sources, education, friends, and personal encounters – all of which are limited, partial, and regularly misleading.

The plausibility of Postema's analysis rests on a widely held assumption that law and society (*necessarily*) form a close fit. As prominent legal historian and sociologist Lawrence Friedman stated, "Legal systems do not float in some cultural void, free of space and time and social context; necessarily, they reflect what is happening in their own societies, like a glove that molds itself to the shape of a person's hand" (Friedman 1996: 72). A close congruence of law with society, however, is not empirically guaranteed because the dis-embeddedness of law declaring institutions entails that the connection between officially recognized law and prevailing social conventions and understandings is always contingent.

An account of how law works in society is called for that drops the assumption that law primarily functions through guiding social behavior. The efficacy of state law in modern societies does not primarily operate through guiding social actors. In the first instance, law guides legal officials and lawyers engaged in legal activities, and it guides people (and entities) who consult lawyers prior to engaging in conduct. The primary contexts in which law guides conduct are substantial commercial transactions and law-related governmental actions, both of which regularly (though not always) involve the participation of lawyers beforehand. Otherwise, for the overwhelming bulk of people engaging in everyday actions, law does not guide their conduct.

In advanced capitalist societies, law mainly functions by constituting a background infrastructure undergirding cultural, social, economic, and political actions. This relatively fixed legal fabric – albeit constantly altered and added to – within which social intercourse occurs has evolved over time interconnected within society (Tamanaha 2017: 139–42). This legal fabric has been woven and rewoven continuously over time through innumerable actions of legal officials enacting, declaring, and applying law and countless lawyers engaging in routine legal activities on behalf of clients (drafting contracts, bringing cases, challenging existing law, etc.). The aggregate result of these actions constitutes contexts within which action takes place, as Postema suggests in his discussion of constitutive mode, but this does not amount to direct or indirect guidance because the legal fabric consists of *legal* arrangements, institutions, and practices, not the *social* practices Postema identifies. Cultural, social, economic, and political practices and institutions are intertwined with the background legal infrastructure, all interconnected, which gradually developed by accretion like thousand-year-old coral reefs integrated with the marine life that surrounds it.

This legal infrastructure functions effectively as a backdrop for societal intercourse notwithstanding that people lack knowledge about the actual details of law and regularly hold incorrect beliefs about law. People carry on with their daily activities simply assuming that appropriate legal rules exist to protect their rights. People routinely sign apartment or car leases, enter employment contracts, purchase chattel, get married, go to a doctor or mechanic for services, click "yes" to contractual agreements for programs downloaded from the internet, and so on – all without reading or fully understanding the legal documents or consulting lawyers beforehand about the legal implications of their actions. Contracts are filled with pages of turgid, nonnegotiable, boilerplate terms written in legalese that laypeople would not fully grasp. People do not look up products liability law before buying a product that they might be injured by or negligence law on proximate cause before getting into a car (or read the details of their insurance contracts and contract law). Even if they tried to find the law, it would be hard to locate without a lawyer because common law doctrines in the USA are not published in authoritative legal texts (the best source of information is a compilation of pattern jury instructions for a given state, which is not itself official law). People do not typically examine the criminal code and civil law before committing fraud or assaulting someone. And they would not fully understand the law even if they did find it.

Innumerable relationships in society are legally structured through largely nonnegotiable form contracts – buyers-sellers, employers-employees, lenders-borrowers, and so on. Contractual details written in legal jargon incorporate terms desired by the dominant party to the transaction (employer, phone company, insurance company, bank, lessor, etc.), along with minimum requirements imposed through government rules and regulations. What the transacting parties focus on are matters like price, quantity, wages, and so on. The purchase of a house, for example, takes place in most states without the immediate participation of an attorney. Present at the closing will be the title company agent to verify the deed, an escrow agent who effects the transfer when both sides have complied with their requirements, a notary, perhaps a representative of the bank to complete the execution of the mortgage, and the real estate broker to collect a check for arranging the sale. The empty spaces on the standardized legal documents that effectuate the transaction are filled in without lawyers – and typically neither the buyer nor the seller read the details of the multipage documents (which they wouldn't understand and cannot alter) beyond verifying the correct address, purchase price, and mortgage amount. As these examples show, law is a backdrop for daily interactions in modern mass societies even when the (obscure) content of the law is not factored into the practical reasoning of the people involved. These are aspects of the taken-for-granted, objectively existing institutions that make up our socially constructed world.

What people *do* know are basic points in broad outline (the socially shared generalized other): property is protected; police can be called when trouble arises (though many African Americans in the USA have a more wary perspective of police than whites); prosecutors bring criminal cases; and so forth. At a personal level, people know they can sue and be sued, both of which are nerve-wracking, costly, and uncertain in outcome.

Without actually knowing the content of applicable law, people assume that appropriate legal protections are in place should something go wrong. This assumption provides people with a sense of security and certainty, although they may turn out to be incorrect. For the most part, in stable societies with an extensive legal infrastructure, the background provided by law is sufficient because the bulk of intercourse largely works satisfactorily thanks to shared moral and social conventions and economic self-interest. Most people would not think of assaulting or killing another; they generally abide by contracts; and so forth because they consider that behavior morally appropriate and personally beneficial, not specifically because the law requires it. People are fundamentally cooperative social beings (Curry et al. 2019; Henrich 2017; Tomasello 2019). Revealingly, studies across legal systems have found that when things do go wrong and the parties cannot resolve it among themselves, in a substantial percentage of instances, people "lump it," suffering the injury without seeking legal recourse (Engel 2010). Official law in many societies, it appears, not only does not guide ex ante but also is often not involved ex post.

In summary, for highly institutionalized contemporary legal systems, with respect to the vast bulk of routine social, economic, and political intercourse, the content of the law operates ex ante through *guiding legal officials and lawyers* as they construct legal directives, requirements, and arrangements that people are subject to in specific contexts of interaction – although most people most of the time do not know and are *not guided* by the law beyond what they might *assume* the law to be. Things function smoothly because conventional social norms, economic self-interest, and business practices promote cooperative social, economic, and political interaction, facilitated by the generally shared *belief* that the law sets up certain limits and protections. Ex post, the content of the law comes into play when legal officials execute and apply the law to disruptions, transgressions, and so forth.

Many analytical jurisprudents apparently believe it is indubitably true that law guides the conduct of the populace. "That law must in some way serve what Scott Shapiro calls its 'essential guidance function' is undeniably true," Wil Waluchow declaims (Waluchow 2008: 92). But empirical evidence tells us it is *not* necessarily true.

8 The False Social Efficacy Thesis

A close cognate of the guidance function of law is the widely asserted position of analytical jurisprudents that law must be generally obeyed by the populace, which Raz claims "all agree" is a necessary condition of law (Raz 2009b: 43). This is the social efficacy thesis. "The significance of this point is that it brings out that normative systems are existing legal systems because of their impact on the behavior of individuals, because of their role in the organization of social life," he explains (106). Hans Kelsen declared, "a legal order is regarded as valid, if its norms are by and large effective (that is, actually applied and obeyed)" (Kelsen 1967: 212). Hart identified as a necessary condition of the existence of a legal system that "those rules of behavior which are valid according to the system's ultimate criteria of validity must be generally obeyed" (Hart 1994: 116). Jeremy Waldron asserts, "there cannot *be* a legal system in a society unless the great proportion of ordinary members of that society comply with the rules identified as valid by the system's rule of recognition" (Waldron 1999: 184). Postema asserts that a substantial degree of congruence between law and social conventions "that predominate in the society governed by it is a necessary condition of the existence of that legal system" (Postema 2008: 56–57). Raz analogizes this condition to morality: "No morality is the social morality of a population unless it is generally conformed to and accepted by that population" (Raz 2009b: 43). (It is important to inject here that his analogy is inapt because morality, like custom, is directly grounded in and sustained by ongoing social conventions, while dis-embedded law creating institutions depend for their immediate existence on the shared conventions of legal officials, which can produce laws that diverge from general social conventions.)

Although analytical jurisprudents seldom question it, the social efficacy thesis is belied by the empirical reality of many legal systems across the world. First, I must draw out a common assumption within the social efficacy thesis: that the legal system purports to govern society (or citizens or populace) as a *whole*. This assumption is based on the monist notion of the supreme, unified law state with comprehensive authority and efficacy within a territory (Tamanaha 2021: 4–10). John Austin explicitly tied positive law to "state," "country," and "society," defining positive law as the command of a supreme sovereign generally obeyed within society: "If a *determinate* human superior, *not* in the habit of obedience to a like superior, receive *habitual* obedience from the *bulk* of a given society, that determinate superior is sovereign in that society, and the society (including the superior) is a society political and independent" (Austin 1832: 200). Kelsen similarly observed, "to say … that the state is the sovereign legal system means, in particular, that it has the capacity, unrestricted by any higher system, to extend its validity territorially as well as materially" (Kelsen 1992: 100). Referring to "citizens" and "whole society," Hart asserted that a legal system exists when laws are "obeyed by the bulk of the populace" (Hart 1994: 114). "Certainly we should not say that a legal system … exists among a given population unless most of the population do abide by the rules recognized as rules of the society by the secondary rules of the system," Waldron asserts (Waldron 1999: 176). As Joseph Raz put it, "We would regard an institutionalized system as a legal one only if it is necessarily in some respect the most important institutionalized system which can exist in that society" (Raz

2009b: 116). "In a nutshell," he asserts, a legal system is "a system of guidance and adjudication claiming supreme authority within a certain society and therefore, where efficacious, also enjoying such effective authority" (43). This is what I call the monist law state image.

Many philosophical theories of law are constructed on this article of faith: law necessarily is the supreme authority governing the entire society. Repeated with certainty and widespread agreement, this assertion has largely escaped scrutiny. The origins of this cluster of beliefs trace back to the sixteenth and seventeenth centuries, during the early stages of the consolidation of the state system in Europe, influentially articulated in the writings of Bodin and Hobbes (see Tamanaha 2021: 26–36). Prior to this period, law was decentralized, with multiple coexisting forms of law and tribunals (regal, ecclesiastical, baronial, feudal, municipal, village, customary, guild, Roman law of jurists, and more), none of which was supreme and comprehensive over all aspects and all groups within society. "The result was the existence of numerous law communities," Max Weber wrote, "the autonomous jurisdictions of which overlapped, the compulsory, political association being only one such autonomous jurisdiction in so far as it existed at all" (Weber 1978: 697). Contrary to the notion of supreme state law governing a territory, going back to classical times, "the personality principle was dominant" (van den Bergh 1969: 343). "In the first place the law of the tribe was personal. It followed the person wherever he traveled or resided. Law, like religion, was a personal possession" (Guterman 1966: 71–72). Weber explained, "in the medieval Imperium, every man was entitled everywhere to be judged by that tribal law by which he 'professed' to live" (Weber 1978: 696).

Declarations by analytical jurisprudents about the social efficacy thesis are drawn from assumptions about nineteenth-century (Austin) and twentieth-century (Hart, Raz, etc.) state legal systems. But, even today, this cluster of monist beliefs about law is demonstrably false. Many existing legal systems past and present fail to meet the purportedly necessary condition that the populace must generally obey the law.

A few pages after declaring the general social obedience requirement, Hart mentions a situation that blatantly refutes it (apparently unbeknownst to him). At the time, the transition from British colonial rule to independence was beginning to take place around the globe. He wrote:

> At a beginning of a period we may have a colony with a local legislature, judiciary, and executive. This constitutional structure has been set up by a statute of the United Kingdom Parliament, which retains full legal competence for the colony . . . . At this stage *the legal system of the colony is plainly a subordinate part of a wider system characterized by the ultimate rule of*

recognition that what the Queen in Parliament enacts is law for (inter alia) the colony. At the end of the period of development the rule of recognition has shifted . . . . The legal system in the former colony has now a 'local root' in that the rule of recognition specifying the ultimate criteria of legal validity no longer refers to the enactments of a legislature of another territory.

(Hart 1994: 120, emphasis added)

When Hart penned this passage, the British Gold Coast, in separate legal acts in 1957 and 1960, achieved complete independence from British colonial rule, becoming Ghana. The ultimate rule of recognition of the legal system that governed the native populace of the British Gold Coast during almost a century of colonial rule, Hart tells us, consisted of social conventions followed by British legal officials in England. This is an extreme instance of a legal system dis-embedded from the society it purports to govern.

What Hart omits to mention is that during British colonial rule across Africa, Asia, and the Pacific, the *legal rules enacted by colonial legal systems were not the rules generally obeyed by the bulk of the populace* in their daily social intercourse. The colonial state imposed transplanted systems of taxation, property, commercial, and criminal law centered on enforcing and facilitating the economic exploitation of native labor and natural resources and advancing the interests of the colonial state and expatriate settlers and their economic enterprises (plantations, mines, etc.) (Tamanaha 2021). "Colonial rule created new 'crimes,' many of which were offences against the imposed structure of colonial management" (Killingray 1986: 413). Employment contracts with native laborers working for expatriate-owned enterprises were enforced by criminal penalties for "desertion," as well as "neglect of duties, negligence, and refusal to work" (Chanock 1992: 294). "The criminal punishing of defaulting workers was one of the major occupations of the colonial courts" (293). Historian C. A. Bayly writes, "In areas of European settlement, these new definitions of property rights could become blunt instruments to bludgeon the weak. They made it possible for white settlers, and sometimes for indigenous elites, to expropriate the common land and labor of the original inhabitants" (Bayly 2003: 112). "The picture is one of a population subject to extensive regulation imposed by laws, the content of which they did not know, and randomly administered by officials, both white and African, who combined administrative and judicial roles" (Chanock 1992: 284–85).

A British-staffed court system was established in the cities and trading centers that applied statutes imposed by the British parliament on colonies, colonial legislation, and common law and equity; local customary law was given limited recognition in state court; and a number of so-called Native Courts were created in district centers to apply customary law among natives. Outside this official state legal system, in vast rural expanses where the overwhelming majority of people lived, unofficial, traditional village tribunals continued to function, applying unwritten customary laws of land tenure, personal injuries, marraige, inheritance, agreements, witchcraft, and so on, to deal with everyday matters of the bulk of the population – utilizing legal norms radically different from transplanted colonial law. Embedded within their way of life, these informal systems of customary law had existed for centuries prior to colonial rule and continued in much the same fashion during colonial rule. The colonial state lacked the institutional capacity to handle local disputes, which were outside its narrow focus on maintaining the power of the colonial state and advancing its extractive economic interests. On their part, indigenous people generally did not resort to colonial courts and did not by and large obey the norms of the colonial legal system for the plain reasons that state legal norms and procedures took place in a language they did not understand and enacted and enforced legal norms alien to their way of life; state courts were also distant, costly, and slow in contrast to informal village tribunals. Hart's purportedly necessary condition that people generally obey the law is not satisfied when people are substantially oblivious to what law requires and they utilize a wholly different set of legal rules to arrange their social life.

Three points bear emphasis about these situations. First, colonial legal systems were *doubly* dis-embedded: in the standard sense that specialized legal institutions manned by legal officials created law and in the more profound sense that the norms and procedures of a legal system that had evolved interconnected within European societies were transplanted to vastly different societies with their own preexisting forms of law and ways of life. Under these conditions, official law could not possibly be congruent with or coincide with social behavior. Second, in these societies, at least two distinct (and often more) socially constructed forms of law existed: state law enforced in state courts collectively recognized by colonial authorities as well as by the population and customary law in traditional tribunals collectively recognized by people in the community (and sometimes by colonial authorities). Third, colonial and postcolonial situations did not resemble civil war, revolution, or enemy occupation, examples which Hart, Kelsen, and Raz discuss as temporary transitional or "half-way stages," during which the existence of a legal system is contested or unresolved (Hart 1994: 118). Rather, these pluralistic legal formations have functioned for over a century in many locations around the globe and by all indications will continue for generations to come (Tamanaha 2021).

The World Bank Legal Department depicts the current situation, a half-century after decolonization:

In many developing countries, customary systems operating outside of the state regime are often the dominant form of regulation and dispute resolution, covering up to 90% of the population in parts of Africa. In Sierra Leone, for example, approximately 85% of the population falls under the jurisdiction of customary law, defined under the Constitution as "the rules which, by custom, are applicable to particular communities in Sierra Leone." Customary tenure covers 75% of land in most African countries, affecting 90% of land transactions in countries like Mozambique and Ghana ... . In many of these countries, systems of justice seem to operate almost completely independently of the official state system. (Chirayath et al. 2005: 3)

It is not just that these informal customary systems operate outside the official legal system but also that the norms of state law and customary law differ on fundamental matters, including land tenure rules, marriage, inheritance, and others, and people arrange their affairs through the latter. "The customary legal framework is not seen as law at all, but as a way of life, how people live – State law on the other hand is something imposed and foreign" (Harper 2011: 28). Customary law and tribunals are collectively recognized and constituted by people within the community as *their* law, which they socially construct through their meaningful beliefs and actions. As legal anthropologist Gordon Woodman put it, "For those communities, customary law is their social life .... Now as always they live it" (Woodman 2011: 30). Many of these are socially embedded forms of law, not controlled by institutionalized legal officials.

Analytical jurisprudents might argue the social efficacy thesis is still satisfied when state law explicitly recognizes customary law, so in that sense, the norms of customary law are state legal norms through incorporation. There are four problems with this response. First, official state recognition (on paper) puts the best face on a situation that the state legal system cannot eliminate without sustained repression of customary law, which it typically lacks the capacity to abolish or replace. Second, the norms of state law and customary law frequently conflict in ways that cannot be reconciled; many people perceive state law and customary law as coexisting alternatives, not as a single integrated legal system. Third, in many of these situations, traditional village tribunals are *not* officially recognized by the legal system, yet they are heavily utilized by people to resolve their disputes (Forsyth 2007). Fourth, situations exist in which the state not only does not recognize but is also actively at war with other forms of law on the same territory, although they coexist for lengthy periods; until the recent takeover by the Taliban, for example, the Afghan state legal system operated within the cities, while centuries-old customary law operated in many rural areas (*jirgas* and *shuras*), and Sharia law was imposed in other areas by Taliban rebels fighting the state. "For ordinary people and villagers, who form the majority of the populace, tribal/customary and Islamic law are more significant and actually better known than any state legislation" (Yassari and Saboory 2010: 273).

John Searle acknowledged that people within communities can collectively recognize property rights (among others) that are contrary to state law. This is common in rural communities that follow customary land tenure as well as in peri-urban areas across the Global South, where as much as 50 percent of people own land and engage in transactions without official titles. "The owners of property are in effect squatters, in the sense that they do not legally own the property, yet they live in a society where their status function is acknowledged and generally recognized and hence, on my account, continues to exist and generate deontic powers [as land owner]," Searle writes (Searle 2006: 22). He is correct to acknowledge the constitutive reality of unofficial property rights, though to call them "squatters" presupposes the state law position; in many of these contexts, those who occupy the land are collectively recognized by the community as legal owners who control the use and disposition of the land. A direct implication of social constructionism is that law exists whenever a community collectively constitutes law through their shared beliefs and practices, notwithstanding that state legal officials might claim a purported monopoly over law.

The social efficacy thesis espoused by Austin, Kelsen, Hart, Raz, Waldron, Postema, and many other legal philosophers is refuted by these situations. The error is not the claim that law must be efficacious (more on this shortly) but the assertion that the bulk of the populace, or citizens, or society must generally obey the law, which is tied to the image of the monist law state controlling a territory. Sweeping declarations by analytical jurisprudents along these lines reflect a lack of awareness of the extent to which this does not hold across the globe. Joseph Raz, for example, declared, "One of the most important facts that made state law central in life as well as in theory is that with all their faults and with all due acknowledgement of exceptions and reservations, states have engendered over their history a strong sense of identity and loyalty among their inhabitants" (Raz 2017: 162). This sweeping assertion assumes that what holds in the contemporary West is normal and representative (a common error committed by analytical jurisprudents). But, in many postcolonial societies across the Global South, state legal institutions are not central in social life, nor do inhabitants have a strong sense of identity with the state. This is not an exceptional or marginal situation. An estimated 57 percent of the global population live in societies with both customary law and state law (Holzinger et al. 2016: 469).

Attempting to account for these situations, Thomas Adams reformulates the existence condition of law as follows: "[W]e can say that a legal system will count as effective if most of its laws are either obeyed, enforced, or *otherwise stand capable of being enforced*" (Adams 2020: 240). Thus, even if the bulk of the populace does not obey the law, the legal system is still efficacious, and therefore exists, if it *could* enforce the law to generate general social conformity, though it may choose not to. But this reformulation falls short as well. In many of these situations past and present, state legal institutions lack the capacity to enforce state legal norms, particularly on rural communities that structure their lives through socially embedded customary law. The colonial state was too weak to extend its legal authority throughout society, though it nonetheless claimed such authority. Since independence, limited progress has been made in bolstering the severely underdeveloped governmental and legal institutions inherited from colonial rule. (With a population of 7.5 million, for example, Rwanda in the early 2000s was served by about 50 lawyers, 20 prosecutors, and 50 newly recruited judges; Malawi had 300 lawyers for 9 million people (Piron 2006: 275, 291).) Seeking to consolidate law in the state, several newly independent states officially abolished customary law and village tribunals, which nevertheless continued to function because state legal systems could not suppress them nor fill the gap that would result. Many weak states exist today that would fail Adam's criteria because they lack the capacity to enforce state law on substantial portions of the population (see Blattman et al. 2014; Giraudy 2012; Rotberg 2013).

To hold onto the social efficacy thesis for society as a whole, analytical jurisprudents might assert that colonial and postcolonial legal systems that fail to meet the condition are *not legal systems*. Elaborating on Hart's requirement that the populace generally obey the law, Jan Mihal specifies that law "causally contributes to social order and peace, [and] does so by means of being known and obeyed" (Mihal 2021: 22). These conditions for the existence of law are justified, he argues, because "our concept of law assumes an important causal relationship between law and society" (31). Legal systems in which these conditions are not satisfied "describes a system which can very plausibly be said not to be law (properly so-called)" (27). Under this analysis, an extraordinary number of colonial and postcolonial legal systems past and present would be philosophically deemed *not law*. Before accepting a conclusion so at odds with the reality of law on the ground, it would make sense instead to reevaluate the soundness of the social efficacy thesis. If significant counterexamples like this do not prompt reconsideration, philosophical assertions of this sort would appear to be virtually immune to empirical refutation, a stance analytical jurisprudents must explain.

Analytical jurisprudents, as this discussion shows, are committed to the assumption that a legal system can exist only if the bulk of the populace generally obeys its norms (or the state has the power to compel them to obey). At bottom, the primary basis to support this position is that it is purportedly entailed within "our" concept of law (which they deem the "central case" of law). But why should our concept of law prevail over the social reality of law? Contemporary analytical jurisprudents have evaluated theories of law through debates about societies of angels (see Miotto 2021) while paying scant attention to manifestations of law around the world that differ profoundly from the Western legal systems upon which their theories of law are grounded. What they apparently fail to realize is that the monist law state image is a self-aggrandizing ideological construct used to bolster the claimed supreme, monopolistic, comprehensive authority of state law over society. Analytical jurisprudents should critically scrutinize the basis, content, and weight they accord to what they claim is "our" concept of law, or the "central case" of law, when declaring philosophical truths about the nature of law.

A final seminal insight revealed by these situations bears on Hart's argument about the minimum content of law: "We can say, given the setting of natural facts and aims, which make sanctions both possible and necessary in a municipal system, that this is a *natural necessity*; and some such phrase is needed also to convey the status of the minimum forms of protection for persons, property, and promises which are *similarly indispensable features of municipal law*" (Hart 1994: 199, emphasis added). Hart was right that natural human traits give rise to basic rules on persons, property, and promises, though he should have added family relations (marriage, divorce, child responsibility, and succession), which are universal, albeit with vast variations and changes in content across societies and over time. Hart made an unwarranted additional supposition, however, when he asserted that these rules are indispensable features of state law. State legal rules commonly include these rules, to be sure, but colonial and postcolonial legal systems reveal that these bodies of rules can be foregone by state law as long as they are supplied by other forms of law. Colonial states created a de facto division of labor involving two distinct forms of law: state law for government and commerce and non-state customary law for the rules of social intercourse of the majority of the populace.

The error of analytical jurisprudents, to be clear, is not the assertion that legal systems must be effective to exist. Law must have some effect in the social arena. State legal systems in postcolonial societies operate mainly in relation to government initiatives, major commercial activities, and in urban centers. Their existence as legal systems is a social fact, notwithstanding that many people, particularly in rural areas, follow collectively recognized socially embedded systems of customary law. The error lies in the notion that legal systems by nature are supreme, unified, and hold a monopoly over law in a society. This is not a conceptual or empirical truth about law but an idealization that legal philosophers ensconce in their theories of law brought in through assertions about "our" concept of law.

9 Missteps in the Quest to Answer "What Is Law?"

The very first sentence of Hart's *The Concept of Law* announces, "Few questions concerning human society have been asked with such persistence and answered by serious thinkers in so many diverse, strange, and even paradoxical ways as the question 'What is law?'" (Hart 1994: 1). What fuels this disagreement, Hart explained, first, is that primitive law and international law, though "conventionally" recognized as law, are "doubtful cases" because they lack legislatures, courts are not mandatory, and no effective system of sanctions exists (3–4). Second, "it is not a peculiarity of complex terms like 'law' and 'legal system' that we are forced to recognize both clear standard cases and challengeable borderline cases"; "that this distinction must be made in the case of almost every general term which we use in classifying features of human life and of the world in which we live" (4). A municipal legal system is "the standard case of what is meant by 'law' and 'legal system'," at least for an educated man, Hart asserted (4–5).

Hart constructs his analysis of law on a series of presuppositions, which he held without examination or justification. These presuppositions had determinative consequences not only for the theory of law he produced but also for subsequent generations of legal philosophers who tread the same path. The first presupposition involves *whose* concept of law determines the starting point of the analysis. Had the question been posed to villagers in Africa, Asia, and the Pacific, many would have first said customary law is law and then mentioned state law as well. Why not start with *their* concepts of law? His second presupposition is that *only one* concept of law must provide the basis for the analysis. Educated Britons, if asked by Hart to list what they consider to be law, would likely mention state law and international law. An educated Briton who is a devout Muslim would add Sharia law to the list as well. Why not include *all forms of law* identified by people as the basis for the analysis? His third presupposition assumes that the central case/borderline case is the correct conceptual framework. Why not frame their relationship as *distinct forms* of law rather than as degrees of approximation of a single core phenomenon? Underlying the preceding, Hart presupposed that the question about the nature of law must be answered in the *singular*: "What *is* law?" This very way of posing the question dictates a singular answer, conceptually denying the possibility that more than one form of law can exist, suitable for different social circumstances, each with different characteristics. Why must law be one thing with a single set of essential features?

Once Hart posited the state legal system as the central case, it automatically followed that any other form of law that does not share the features of state law would be deemed "pre-legal," at the borders, or not law. If instead he has posited customary law, state law, and international law as his set of what counts as law, the features of law he identified would have been different; alternatively, he might have considered each a distinct form of law with its own characteristic features (cf. Waldron 2013). Foregoing these alternatives without consideration of their merits decisively narrowed the path of analytical jurisprudence.

Lately, analytical jurisprudents have begun to take seriously other forms of law (Roughan and Halpin 2017). The rise of globalization and increasing penetration of international law into the domain of sovereign states prompted Joseph Raz to ask: "Will state law retain its standing as the paradigm of law, and as the focus of legal philosophy?" (Raz 2017: 155). The "exclusive concentration on the state was, it now turns out, never justified, and is even less justified today," he concluded (161). Turning philosophical attention to other forms of law promises to fundamentally alter theorizing about the concept of law and law as a social institution.

When they consider manifestations of law besides state law, analytical jurisprudents can learn from social scientific theorizing about law. "To seek a definition of law is like the quest for the Holy Grail," wrote legal anthropologist Adam Hoebel mid-century (Hoebel 1946: 839). After decades of efforts by many sophisticated theorists, this quest was finally abandoned. Essential lessons about law can be gleaned from their lack of success. As I show below, analytical jurisprudents in recent years have repeated the same missteps that foiled social scientists. A formidable dual-sided problem that defeats efforts to define law or to identify the essential features of law are the pitfalls of over- and under-inclusiveness. For reasons I explain, all form- and function-based theories of law unavoidably suffer from one or the other or both.

Every theory of law starts by positing what counts as law, which predetermines the theory of law produced. This circularity does not undermine the analysis, but it tells us that the initial choice of paradigm is critical and must be justified. Contemporary analytical jurisprudents uniformly begin with state law because that is the dominant form of law in their societies. Legal anthropologists used a different approach because state law was not predominant in the societies they studied. Instead, they observed familiar legal phenomena (responses to disputes over property, injuries, sexual relations, agreements, etc.) and worked from that basis to identify features of law. These forms of law were embedded within society without differentiated legal institutions. Hoebel's criteria for law encompasses informal tribunals – composed of respected elders, for example – applying customary law that rendered decisions carried out by members of the community: "A social norm is legal if its neglect or infraction is regularly met, in threat or in fact, by the application of physical force by an individual or group possessing the socially recognized privilege of so acting" (Hoebel 2006: 28). Law can exist under this definition even in the absence of a differentiated legal system when no system of secondary rules exists. The point here is not that his definition is correct but that his alternative starting point is theoretically justifiable and results in a different account of law's defining features.

Theories of law produced by philosophers and social scientists can be grouped into two basic categories (with many variations of each): those based on the social ordering function of law and those that reduce law to institutionalized rule systems. The two leading theorists of the first category, writing early in the twentieth century in very different contexts, are pioneering legal sociologist Eugen Ehrlich and legal anthropologist Bronislaw Malinowski. Ehrlich observed first hand that law actually followed within communities in multiethnic Bukovina frequently departed from the Austrian Civil Code. In contrast to legislation and judicial decisions (which he called "rules for decision"), Ehrlich identified the "living law" as the rules actually followed in social associations, including families, businesses, professions, factories, and so forth (Ehrlich 1936: 493). Living among the Trobriand Islanders in Melanesia, Malinowski observed that they had law on basic matters of social intercourse (property, marriage, etc.), which were invoked in the resolution of disputes.

Both denied that law necessarily requires legal institutions. The living law, Ehrlich emphasized, is lived social ordering that does not necessarily take the same institutionalized form as state law:

> It is not an essential element of the concept of law that it be created by the state, nor that it constitute the basis for the decisions of the courts or other tribunals, nor that it be the basis of a legal compulsion consequence upon such a decision. A fourth element remains, and that will have to be the point of departure, i.e. the law is an ordering. (Ehrlich 1936: 24)

Malinowski made the same point when he contested the position that law consists of "central authority, codes, courts, and constables" (Malinowski 1926: 14); to the contrary, law "does not consist in any independent institution" (59).

Ehrlich and Malinowski's conceptions of law are similar in core respects. Law for both was embedded in social life. Both identify law through observation of "concrete usages," with law consisting of what "the parties actually observe in life" (Ehrlich 1936: 493) – discernable by attention to how "they function in actual life" (Malinowski 1926: 125). "Law represents rather an aspect of their tribal life, one side of their structure, than any independent, self-contained social arrangement," Malinowski observed (59). Both point to reciprocity, positive incentives, and social obligations as primary forces behind binding law, denying that physical coercion is necessary to law. As Ehrlich put it, "A man therefore conducts himself according to law, chiefly because this is made imperative by his social relations" (Ehrlich 1936: 75). Similarly, Malinowski wrote, "The binding forces of Melanesian civil law are to be found in the concatenation of the obligations, in the fact that they are arranged into chains of mutual services, a give and take extending over long periods of time and covering wide aspects of interest and activity" (Malinowski 1926 67). People follow the law mainly owing to a normative agreement and positive inducement, mutual dependence, a sense of reciprocal obligations woven into relationships, and social ostracism and potential loss of future benefits from non-compliance, but not mainly due to fear of physical coercion, though that could be a factor as well.

Both theories of law have been widely criticized for failing to distinguish law from other aspects of social life. Legal philosopher Morris Cohen wrote at the time, "Ehrlich's book suffers from the fact that it draws no clear account of what he means by law and how he distinguishes it from customs and morals" (Cohen 1916: 537). Jurisprudent Felix Cohen objected that "under Ehrlich's terminology, law itself merges with religion, ethical custom, morality, decorum, tact, fashion, and etiquette" (Cohen 1937: 1130). "The conception of law that Malinowski propounded was so broad that it was virtually indistinguishable from a study of the obligatory aspect of all social relationships," objected legal anthropologist Sally Falk Moore. "Law is not distinguished from social control in general" (1969: 258). Simon Roberts critically remarked, "Although Malinowski uses the term 'law' here, he seems to employ it so widely as to embrace all modes of social control" (Roberts 1976: 674). This is the problem of over-inclusiveness.

The source of over-inclusiveness was mentioned earlier: functional equivalents. A sociological commonplace is that virtually all social functions can be served in alternative ways (Merton 1957); criteria based on function alone draw in all functional equivalents. Ehrlich and Malinowski saw the function of law as social ordering, and they observed what appeared to be familiar legal norms followed by people in their social intercourse within groups (property, personal injuries, agreements, marriage, etc.). Ehrlich saw that these norms were often different from or provided sources for official state law; Malinowski saw that differentiated legal institutions did not exist among the Trobriand. What was plain to both theorists was that these legal norms were maintained by social relations (conventions, moral norms, expectations, reciprocity, etc.), not by differentiated legal institutions exerting force. These studies are reminders that official legal systems are not the only social mechanism that maintains social order. Over-inclusiveness results because anything defined in terms of a function – social ordering – encompasses all phenomena that help maintain that function – customs, morality, reciprocity, and so on.

Now let us examine the second category of concepts of law. Theorists who construct law in this category invariably posit state law as the paradigm of law then reduce law by paring away non-essential features. This results in criteria that match state law's combination of institutionalized form/structure and function. That explains why "[m]any, if not all, legal philosophers have been agreed that one of the defining features of law is that it is an institutional normative system," Raz asserts (Raz 2009b: 105). Thus, for Hart, law consists of institutionalized systems (form) that recognize, change, and apply norms in social ordering (function). Shapiro reduced law to a "self-certifying compulsory planning organization [form] whose aim is to solve those moral problems that cannot be solved, or solved as well, through alternative forms of social ordering [function]" (Shapiro 2011: 224).

A pivotal conceptual consequence of defining law in terms of an institutionalized system is that "law" and "legal system" are construed as interchangeable equivalents. "Such is the standard case of what is meant by 'law' and 'legal system'," Hart wrote, merging the two (Hart 1994: 5). Shapiro pronounces it a self-evident truism that "Laws are always members of legal system" (2011: 15). Equating law with legal system is pivotal because it conceptually precludes the possibility that forms of law can exist that are not institutionalized systems. Raz drew this conclusion while treating them interchangeably: "When surveying the different forms of social organization in different societies throughout the ages we will find many which resemble the law in various ways. Yet if they lack the essential features of the law, they are not legal systems" (Raz 2009a: 25). John Gardner explained the consensus view: "Law, understood as a genre of artefacts, is a genre made up of systems of norms together with the norms that belong to those systems" (Gardner 2004: 171).

The requirement that law is an institutionalized rule system creates the problem of *under*-inclusiveness. Any form of law that does not possess the institutionalized structure of state law is disqualified. That is why Hart concluded that primitive law and international law are not law but prelegal. This theory is under-inclusive because it rejects what many people consider to be law – generating howls of protest by international lawyers against Hart's theory of law.

We have drilled down to a major reason for perennial disagreement over theories of law. Any theorist who believes customary law and international law *are* law must reject any theory of law grounded on the institutional structure of state law (which they do not fully possess); conversely, any theorist who believes state law is *the* paradigm of law must include the institutional structure of state law. There is no way to combine these two positions in a single concept of law. Only by superseding the clash can both sides be given their due.

This second category of theories of law solves the Ehrlich–Malinowski problem by successfully distinguishing law from customs and morals, which are not usually recognized and enforced by standing institutions, but it also suffers from *over*-inclusiveness (Tamanaha 2017: 43–53). Society is filled with institutionalized rule systems that recognize, apply, and enforce norms in ways that help maintain social order (corporations, sports leagues, state law, etc.); there are numerous organized planning systems whose aim is to solve complex moral problems (churches, charities, state law, etc.). State law is included by these combinations of form and function, but so are multitudes of other institutionalized rule systems. Once again, the existence of functional equivalents is the source of over-inclusiveness – anything that matches the specified combination of form and function is encompassed as law.

Legal sociologist Marc Galanter revealed this implication four decades ago when he enlisted Hart's union of primary and secondary rules to conclude that law "can be found in a variety of institutional settings – *universities, sports leagues, housing developments, hospitals,* etc" (Galanter 1981: 17–18, emphasis added). Analytical jurisprudents have made similar assertions. In the 1990s, Neil MacCormick identified "the 'living law' of social associations like *universities, firms or families* (all of which seem to me to work, when they do, in terms of what is at least partly institutionalized normative order)" (MacCormick 1993: 14, emphasis added). "But state law is not the only kind of law that there is. There is also law between states, international law, and law of organized association of states such as the EC/EU, law of churches and other religious unions or communities, laws of games and *laws of national and international sporting associations,*" he reiterated (MacCormick 1995: 261, emphasis added). Joseph Raz recently echoed these statements:

> Even though much of legal philosophy takes state law as its starting point, writers are aware of the existence of other kinds of law, and I do not mean laws of nature, mathematics, or grammar. I mean laws that are uncontroversially

> normative. They include international law, or the law of organizations like the
> European Union but also Canon Law, Sharia law, Scottish law, the law of native
> nations, *the rules and regulations governing the activities of voluntary associ-*
> *ations, or those of legally recognized corporations, and more, including many*
> *very transient phenomena, like neighborhood gangs.*
>
> (Raz 2017:138, emphasis added)

He continued: "In this sense, both the rules of the Roman Republic and those of
the University of Wales (disbanded 2011), just as the rules of the United States
and of Columbia University, *are* legal systems" (143, emphasis added). Shapiro
similarly acknowledged this implication, with a hedge, noting that "the United
States Golf Association ... straddles the line between law and non-law"
(Shapiro 2011: 224).

  Institutionalized rule systems are ubiquitous in society because rules are
fundamental to human social interaction, and institutionalization is an effective
way to organize and carry out bodies of rules. Their pervasiveness is
a manifestation of the repetition of useful functional arrangements in social
life. Legal theorists who assert that universities and sports leagues *are law*
conflate a particular version of rule system (legal systems) with the entire
category of institutionalized rule systems. What they have done, in effect, is
relabel institutionalized rule systems as "law."

  The error in this analysis is revealed by John Searle's ontology of social
institutions. Searle elaborates, "The ontology I have given [for government or
state] so far might also fit nonpolitical structures such as *religions, corpor-*
ations, universities, and organized sports" (Searle 2010: 170, emphasis added).
The legal theorists quoted previously cite precisely the same examples as "law";
Searle, however, does not present these as law but rather as phenomena that
share a common institutional rule structure. His point is that beneath the surface
are "purely formal features that they have in common that enable them to
function in human life" (123). Searle does not offer a theory of law, though he
observes that what "distinguishes governments from churches, universities, ski
clubs, and marching bands" is that "it maintains a constant threat of physical
force" (171).

  What these legal theorists have identified as law's essential features, to
repeat, are not law per se but institutionalized rule systems, a broad and diverse
set that (state) law is a member of but not the entire set. Over-inclusiveness
results when they use the term law for all other members of the set of institutionalized rule systems. Michael Giudice's recent argument that law has
a necessary natural core illustrates this problem. He calls this core "social
source normativity." Social source normativity is "the idea that the mere fact
that a rule, norm, or standard has been created or accepted, or a particular order

or directive issued, itself serves or can serve as a reason to do or not do something, *independently of the content or merits of* the rule, norm, and so on" (Giudice 2020: 92). "Parents, social groups, priests, judges, parliaments, and so on, are all social (that is, impersonal) sources of content-independent normativity, as they can all issue or create norms for others (and sometimes themselves) to follow" (93). Giudice would be on solid ground if he had asserted that social source normativity is an aspect of created *rules*, and since law consists of created rules, it is an aspect of law. However, he goes beyond this to assert that "law exists wherever and whenever we find social source normativity" (95). Over-inclusiveness follows because this stance turns all created rules into law; he writes, "if law is indeed a basic, natural phenomenon, then we ought not to be surprised to find it in various social situations, beginning even with the simple rules of children's games" (96).

Appending additional criteria to distinguish law does not solve these problems because theorists must contend with the dual dilemmas of over- and under-inclusiveness. Mihal, for example, attempts to avoid the overinclusiveness of Hart's theory by adding the requirement that a legal system's "valid rules causally contribute to social order and peace" of society as a whole (Mihal 2021: 1, 14). This helps narrow the category, eliminating rule systems like sports leagues, which do not contribute to social order and peace of society, but it also compounds under-inclusiveness. Since Mihal retains Hart's institutional structure, informal customary law is not law, and in addition, magnifying under-inclusiveness, colonial and postcolonial legal systems are not law because they do not causally maintain the order of the whole society. Mihal's theory of law disqualifies a multitude of legal phenomena that have been collectively recognized as law by hundreds of millions of people past and present.

Each prong of this dual-sided problem identifies a distinct flaw in theories of law. Under-inclusiveness arises because the paradigm of law was restricted to state law, excluding customary law, religious law, and international law. The many people who collectively recognize these other forms of law object that the theory of law is wrong because it denies the legal status of their form of law. The objection of under-inclusiveness exposes the assumption that state law provides the sole, authoritative paradigm for what counts as law. The objection of overinclusiveness exposes that the process of theoretical abstraction lost touch with the initial object of analysis. The claim that institutionalized rule systems like universities and sports leagues *are law* would strike most people as strange. Legal philosophers who take this position commit a category mistake: it is not that all institutionalized rule systems are law but that (state) law is one type of institutionalized rule system. It is not possible to construct an exclusively form- and function-based account of law that escapes the problems of over- and under-inclusiveness.

Objections of under- and over-inclusiveness arise when the theory of law conflicts with common intuitions about what law is. This raises the question: Why should common intuitions be a standard for evaluating the soundness of a theory of law? Analytical jurisprudents might respond that these common intuitions are wrong, lay confusions exposed and corrected by legal philosophers. Understood philosophically, customary law and international law are *not law* (Hart), while the rules of universities and sports leagues *are law* (MacCormick and Raz). People will apprehend law more astutely if they adopt the sophisticated position of legal philosophers.

This stance is untenable. Common intuitions cannot be dismissed outright as confused because philosophical theories are ultimately grounded on common intuitions about what law is – this is the circularity identified at the outset. Analytical jurisprudents build their analyses on common intuitions, so objections based on common intuitions are valid. Objections of under- and over-inclusiveness raise questions about the starting point and the results of the analysis. Since law is ultimately a folk concept – law is what people conceive of as law – philosophical theories must be judged in relation to common intuitions.

Let me now sketch an alternative way to construct a theory of law that avoids these problems. The starting point to produce a theory of law is to identify what counts as law, assembling the pre-theoretical "data set of law" (Webber 2015: 63). We can begin with Raz's list of examples of law (excluding institutionalized rule systems): "international law, or the law of organizations like the European Union but also Canon Law, Sharia law, Scottish law, the law of native nations" (Raz 2017:138). We can add the state legal systems in Japan, North Korea, Iran, and Israel; Halacha in Jewish communities around the world; Yapese customary law, *Adat* law in Indonesian villages; tribal customary law in rural Afghanistan; and countless other examples. These contemporary instances should be supplemented by historical examples of law, like the law of the Roman Republic, customary law in medieval Europe, colonial legal systems, and so forth.

The data set of law is compiled by including whatever is conventionally identified as law within communities. Law *is* whatever people identify and treat through their social practices as "law" (and its translations, *droit, recht, lex, ius, prawo, falu, derecho, horitsu*, etc.; Tamanaha 2017: 73–77, 2001: 166, 194). This proposal has been met with "almost universal rejection," Andrew Halpin declared (2014: 181), because "it lacks any analytical or explanatory bite." Analytical jurisprudents critical of this position fail to realize, however, that they too (implicitly) rely upon the very same conventionalist approach. Raz came up with the examples of law on his list, as I did, by including what has been conventionally identified as "law." The explanatory basis for this is social constructionism. Conventional recognition accords these phenomena with status as "law" (with attendant legal powers) within the community that recognizes them as such. Andrei Marmor recently articulated a similar conventionalist account: "The most important insight of legal positivism, I think, is the idea that whatever counts as law in a given society is law in that society. And more generally, that there is nothing more to what law is, in terms of its ontological grounding, than that which counts as law where and when it does so count" (Marmor 2018: 19).

A number of implications related to the preceding discussion immediately follow from using the conventional identification of law as a starting point. Under- and over-inclusiveness are avoided: customary law and international law *are* law because there are conventionally seen as such; universities and sports leagues *are not* law because they are not conventionally seen as such. Moreover, the assumption that there is a single standard or central case that determines what counts as law must be set aside (Halpin 2014: 177–80). More than one conventionally identified form of law exists and can be present in a given society, and there is no reason to assume that they must all be conceptually arranged as variations of a central case. The functions of each form of law depend on an examination of what they are used for and what their consequences are. Whether and how each recognized form of law guides social conduct and who obeys them are matters of empirical investigation. All of the philosophical positions questioned in this Element must be examined anew in light of multiple conventionally recognized forms of law.

Once examples of conventionally identified law have been complied, the analytical work begins. One can examine whether these forms of law have shared features or whether they fall into distinct categories each with its own features. This is complicated because categories can be constructed along various lines using various considerations and criteria. The goal is to carve legal phenomena at their joints in the most illuminating fashion. Many other questions of philosophical interest can be examined. Since this is a new path, the possibilities for analytical contemplation of law are wide open.

It is not possible to fully discuss the conventionalist approach I propose, which raises objections that I have taken up elsewhere (Tamanaha 2017). Here, I briefly introduce it to show that alternative approaches exist that avoid the problems identified in this critique. One merit of this proposed alternative, consistent with the theme of this Element, is that it casts a broad net over legal phenomena and draws on empirical information about law.

Philosophy of Law

10 Empiricism and Analytical Jurisprudence

The preceding analysis challenges a number of propositions held by analytical jurisprudents: that legal systems are artifacts, that domination is not a characteristic function of law, that law guides social behavior, that the bulk of citizens must obey law for it to exist, that law is necessarily supreme, that state law is the exclusive paradigm for law, that law and legal system are interchangeable, that law has a singular set of essential and necessary characteristics, that other forms of law are borderline instances of a standard case, and that theories of law can be built on the form and function of law. These positions, I have argued, are in various ways inconsistent with social reality.

Finally, let me address why analytical jurisprudents should care about the points I have raised. Needless to say, philosophical theories of law are not empirical theories. The respective orientations and goals of these intellectual pursuits are different. Analytical jurisprudents seek general propositions about law, fundamental features, common traits, universal truths, and analytical clarifications about the nature of law. Empirical theories of law tend to focus on contingency, variation, change, interconnections, details, and what happens on the ground. Each endeavor has its own value, strengths, and omissions, and neither need answer to the standards and interests of the other. The significant differences between the two, however, do not mean they cannot learn from one another. I regularly consume, learn from, and import analytical insights to sharpen my empirically oriented theoretical work on law. In this Element, I turn the lens in the opposite direction, hoping to benefit analytical jurisprudence, not just on the specific issues I raise but also in demonstrating the value of greater empirical input.

In "The Pursuit of Philosophy," Isaiah Berlin explains that the remit of philosophy has changed over time. Many significant questions once considered philosophical were later taken over by science when it was understood that they could be answered scientifically. Notwithstanding these changes, philosophy has a unique role and contribution to knowledge. "The perennial task of philosophers is to examine whatever seems insusceptible to the methods of the sciences or of everyday observation, for example, categories, concepts, models, ways of thinking or acting, and particularly ways in which they clash with one another, with a view to constructing other, less internally contradictory, and (though this can never be fully attained) less pervertible metaphors, images, symbols and systems of categories" (Berlin 1978, 11). "The goal of philosophy is always the same, to assist men to understand themselves and thus operate in the open, and not wildly, in the dark" (11). Philosophers must be attentive to science not only because certain philosophical speculations have empirical answers but also because, to fulfill its task of illumination, philosophical work built on empirical propositions must strive to get things right. As I quoted earlier, Hart recognized that certain issues he raises "do not rest on truisms" but are for "sociology or psychology like other sciences to establish" (Hart 1961: 190).

Analytical jurisprudents should be open to empiricism because law is a *social institution*. Analytical insights about law as a social institution are grounded on claims about what law is and does, which at bottom *are* empirical propositions. The entire edifice of analytical jurisprudence is built on an empirical foundation. Too often empirical propositions are smuggled in sans empirical support by resorting to intuitions, claims about "self-evident truisms," or bald references to "our" concept of law. What I have tried to demonstrate is that a number of central claims made by analytical jurisprudents are based on falsifiable assumptions, idealizations, or drawn too narrowly in time and place. Theories of law must comport with the social reality of law; if not, they risk devolving into elaborate, untethered, speculative theorizing with limited edificatory value. If analytical jurisprudents aspire to understand the nature of law as a social institution – to enable people to "operate in the open, and not wildly, in the dark" – then philosophical progress will be made by constructing theories of law on an empirically informed base.

References

Adams, Thomas. (2020). "The Efficacy Condition." *Legal Theory* 25: 225–43.

Austin, John. (1832). *The Province of Jurisprudence Determined*. London: John Murray.

Baldwin, D. John. (2002). *George Herbert Mead: A Unifying Theory for Sociology*. Dubuque: Kendall/Hunt.

Bayly, Christopher A. (2003). *The Birth of the Modern World, 1780 – 1914*. Malden: Wiley-Blackwell.

Bentham, Jeremy. (1977). *A Comment on the Commentaries and a Fragment on Government* (J. H. Burns and H. L. A. Hart, eds.). Oxford: Clarendon Press.

Berger, Peter L. and Thomas Luckmann. (1966). *The Social Construction of Reality: A Treatise in the Sociology of Knowledge*. New York: Doubleday.

Berlin, Isaiah. (1978). *Concepts and Categories*. Princeton: Princeton University Press.

Blattman, Christopher, Alexandra C. Hartman, and Robert A. Blair. (2014). "How to Promote Order and Property Rights under Weak Rule of Law? An Experiment in Changing Dispute Resolution Behavior through Community Education." *The American Political Science Review* 108(1): 100–20.

Brown, Donald E. (1991). *Human Universals*. New York: McGraw Hill.

Burazin, Luka. (2016). "Can There be an Artifact Theory of Law?" *Ratio Juris* 29: 385–401.

Burazin, Luka. (2018). "Legal Systems as Abstract Institutional Artifacts." In Luka Burazin, Kenneth Einar Himma, and Corrado Roversi (eds.), *Law as an Artifact*. Oxford: Oxford University Press, 112–35.

Burazin, Luka. (2019a). "Legal Systems, Intentionality, and a Functional Explanation of Law." *Jurisprudence* 10(2): 229–36.

Burazin, Luka. (2019b). "Law as an Artifact." In Mortimer Sellers and Stephan Kirste (eds.), *Encyclopedia of the Philosophy of Law and Social Philosophy*. Dordrecht: Springer.

Chanock, Martin. (1992). "The Law Market: The Legal Encounter in British East and Central Africa." In Wolfgang J. Mommsen and J. A. de Moor (eds.), *European Expansion and Law: The Encounter of European and Indigenous Law in 19th and 20th Century Africa and Asia*. Oxford: Berg, 279–305.

Chirayath, Leila, Caroline Sage, and Michael Woolcock. (2005). *Customary Law and Policy Reform*. Washington, DC: World Bank Legal Department.

Claessen, Henri. (2002). "Was the State Inevitable?" *Social Evolution & History* 1: 101–11.

Cohen, Felix. (1937). "Book Review: Fundamental Principles of the Sociology of Law." *Illinois Law Review* 31: 1128–34.

Cohen, Morris R. (1916). "Recent Philosophical-Legal Literature in French, German and Italian (1912–1914)." *The International Journal of Ethics* 26(4): 528–46.

Comaroff, John L. (1981). *Rules and Processes: The Cultural Logic of Dispute in an African Context*. Chicago: University of Chicago Press.

Cottone, Michael. (2015). "Rethinking Presumed Knowledge of the Law in the Regulatory Age." *Tennessee Law Review* 82(1): 137–66.

Crowe, Jonathan. (2014). "Law as an Artifact Kind." *Monash University Law Review* 40: 737–57.

Curry, Oliver, Daniel Mullins, and Harvey Whitehouse. (2019). "Is it Good to Cooperate? Testing the Theory of Morality-as-Cooperation in 60 Societies." *Current Anthropology* 60(1): 47–69.

Darley, John M., Paul H. Robinson, and Kevin M. Carlsmith. (2001). "The Ex Ante Function of the Criminal Law Papers of General Interest." *Law & Society Review* 35(1): 165–90.

Dewey, John. (1914). "Logical Method and Law." *The Cornell Law Quarterly* 10(1): 17–27.

Dewey, John. (1941). "My Philosophy of Law." In *My Philosophy of Law: Credos of Sixteen American Scholars*. Julius Rosenthal Foundation. Boston: Boston Law Book, 71–85.

Diaz-Leon, Esa. (2013). "What is Social Construction?" *European Journal of Philosophy* 23: 1137–52.

Ehrenberg, Kenneth M. (2015). "Law's Artifactual Nature: How Legal Institutions Generate Normativity." In George Pavlakos and Veronica Rodriguez-Blanco (eds.), *Reasons and Intentions in Law and Practical Agency*. Cambridge: Cambridge University Press, 247–66.

Ehrenberg, Kenneth M. (2016). *The Functions of Law*. Oxford: Oxford University Press.

Ehrenberg, Kenneth M. (2018). "Law is an Institution, an Artifact, and a Practice." In Luka Burazin, Kenneth Einar Himma, and Corrado Roversi (eds.), *Law as an Artifact*. Oxford: Oxford University Press, 177–91.

Ehrenberg, Kenneth M. (2020). "The Institutionality of Legal Validity." *Philosophy and Phenomenological Research* 100(2): 277–301.

Ehrlich, Eugen. (1936). *Fundamental Principles of the Sociology of Law* (Walter Moll, trans.). Cambridge, MA: Harvard University Press.

Elder-Voss, Dave. (2012). *The Reality of Social Construction*. Cambridge: Cambridge University Press.

Engel, David M. (2010–2011). "Lumping as Default in Tort Cases: The Cultural Interpretation of Injury and Causation Symposium: Injuries without Remedies." *Loyola of Los Angeles Law Review* 44(1): 33–68.

Fay, Brian. (1994). "General Laws Explaining Human Behavior." In Michael Martin and Lee C. McIntyre (eds.), *Readings in the Philosophy of Social Science*. Cambridge, MA: MIT Press, 91–110.

Flannery, Kent and Joyce Marcus. (2012). *The Creation of Inequality: How Our Prehistoric Ancestors Set the Stage for Monarchy, Slavery, and Empire*. Cambridge, MA: Harvard University Press.

Forsyth, Miranda. (2007). "A Typology of Relationships between State and Non-State Justice Systems." *Journal of Legal Pluralism and Unofficial Law* 56: 67–112.

Friedman, Jonathan. (2006). "Comment on Searle's 'Social Ontology'." *Anthropological Theory* 6: 70–80.

Friedman, Lawrence M. (1996). "Borders: On the Emerging Sociology of Transnational Law Essay." *Stanford Journal of International Law* 32(1): 65–90.

Galanter, Marc. (1981). "Justice in Many Rooms: Courts, Private Ordering, and Indigenous Law." *The Journal of Legal Pluralism and Unofficial Law* 13(19): 1–47.

Gardner, John. (2004). "The Legality of Law." *Ratio Juris* 17(2): 168–81.

Giraudy, Agustina. (2012). "Conceptualizing State Strength: Moving Beyond Strong and Weak States." *Revista de Ciencia Política* 32(3): 599–611.

Giudice, Michael. (2020). *Social Construction of Law: Potential and Limits*. Northampton: Edward Elgar.

Gorski, Philip S. (2016). "The Matter of Emergence: Material Artifacts and Social Structure." *Qualitative Sociology* 39: 211–15.

Green, Leslie. (1998). "The Functions of Law." *Cogito* 12: 117–24.

Green, Leslie. (2008). "Positivism and the Inseparability of Law and Morals Symposium: The Hart-Fuller Debate at Fifty." *New York University Law Review* 83(4): 1035–58.

Green, Leslie. (2012). "Introduction." In H. L. A. Hart, *The Concept of Law* (Penelope Bulloch and Joseph Raz, eds.), 3rd ed. Oxford: Clarendon Press, xv–iv.

Hadfield, Gillian K. and Joy Heine. (2016). "Law in the Law-Thick World: The Legal Resource Landscape for Ordinary Americans." In Sam Estreicher and Joy Radice (eds.), *Beyond Elite Law: Access to Civil Justice for Ordinary Americans*. New York: Cambridge University Press, 21–52.

Halpin, Andrew. (2014). "The Creation and Use of Concepts of Law when Confronting Legal and Normative Plurality." In Sean P. Donlan and Lucas H. Urscheler (eds.), *Concepts of Law: Comparative, Jurisprudential, and Social Science Perspectives*. Farnham: Ashgate, 169–92.

Harper, Erica. (2011). *Customary Justice: From Program Design to Impact Evaluation*. Rome: IDLO.

Hart, H. L. A. (1961). *The Concept of Law*. Oxford: Clarendon Press.

Hart, H. L. A. (1994). *The Concept of Law* (Penelope Bulloch and Joseph Raz, eds.), 2nd ed. Oxford: Oxford University Press.

Henrich, Joseph. (2017). *The Secret of Our Success: How Culture is Driving Human Evolution, Domesticating Our Species, and Making Us Smarter*. Princeton: Princeton University Press.

Hilpinen, Risto. (2011). "Artifact." In Edward Zalta (ed.), *The Stanford Encyclopedia of Philosophy* (Winter 2011 Edition). https://stanford.library.sydney.edu.au/archives/fall2011/entries/artifact/

Hoebel, E. Adamson (1946). "Law and Anthropology." *Virginia Law Review* 32(4): 835–54.

Hoebel, E. Adamson (2006[1954]). *The Law of Primitive Man: A Study in Comparative Legal Dynamics*. Cambridge, MA: Harvard University Press.

Holmes, Oliver Wendell. (1873). "The Gas Stoker's Strike." *American Law Review* 7: 582.

Holzinger, Katharina, Florian G. Kern, and Daniela Kromrey. (2016). "The Dualism of Contemporary Traditional Governance and the State: Institutional Setups and Political Consequences." *Political Research Quarterly* 69(3): 469–81.

Jhering, Rudolph von. (1914). *Law as a Means to an End. Translated by Issack Husik*. Boston: Boston.

Katz, Larissa M. (2018). "Philosophy of Property Law." In J. Tasioulas (ed.), *Cambridge Companion to the Philosophy of Law*. Cambridge: Cambridge University Press, 371–88.

Kelley, Donald R. (1990). *The Human Measure: Social Thought in the Western Legal Tradition*. Cambridge, MA: Harvard University Press.

Kelsen, Hans. (1967). *Pure Theory of Law*. Translation M. Knight. Berkeley: University of California Press.

Kelsen, Hans. (1992). *An Introduction to the Problems of Legal Theory*. Trans. Bonnie Litschewski Paulson and Stanley L. Paulson. Oxford: Clarendon Press.

Khalid, Muhammad. (2019). "Law as a Social Kind." CEUR-WS 2518, http://ceur-ws.org/Vol-2518/paper-SOLEE3.pdf

Killingray, David. (1986). "The Maintenance of Law and Order in British Colonial Africa." *African Affairs* 85(340): 411–37.

Kim, Pauline T. (1999). "Norms, Learning, and Law: Exploring the Influences on Workers' Legal Knowledge." *University of Illinois Law Review* 1999(2): 447–516.

Lacey, Nicola. (2006). "Analytical Jurisprudence versus Descriptive Sociology Revisited." *Texas Law Review* 84(4): 944–82.

Leiter, Brian. (2011). "The Demarcation Problem in Jurisprudence: A New Case for Skepticism." *Oxford Journal of Legal Studies* 31: 663–77.

MacCormick, Neil. (1993). "Beyond the Sovereign State." *The Modern Law Review* 56(1): 1–18.

MacCormick, Neil. (1995). "The Maastricht-Urteil: Sovereignty Now." *European Law Journal* 1(3): 259–66.

Malinowski, Bronislaw. (1926). *Crime and Custom in Savage Society.* New York: Harcourt, Brace & Company.

Marcoulatos, Iordanis. (2003). "John Searle and Pierre Bourdieu: Divergent Perspectives on Intentionality and Social Ontology." *Human Studies* 26: 67–96.

Marmor, Andrei (2004). "The Rule of Law and Its Limits." *Law and Philosophy* 23(1): 1–43.

Marmor, Andrei. (2007). *Law in the Age of Pluralism.* Oxford: Oxford University Press.

Marmor, Andrei. (2018). *What's Left of General Jurisprudence? On Law's Ontology and Content* (SSRN Scholarly Paper No. ID 3165550), https://papers.ssrn.com/abstract=3165550

Marmor, Andrei. (2019). "The Nature of Law." In Edward N. Zalta (ed.), *Stanford Encyclopedia of Philosophy.* https://plato.stanford.edu/cgi-bin/encyclopedia/archinfo.cgi?entry=lawphil-nature

Mead, George Herbert. (1915). "Natural Rights and the Theory of the Political Institution." *Journal of Philosophy, Psychology, and Scientific Methods* 12: 141–55.

Mead, George Herbert. (1918). "The Psychology of Punitive Justice." *American Journal of Sociology* 23: 577-602.

Mead, George Herbert. (1934). *Mind, Self, and Society.* Chicago: Chicago University Press.

Mead, George Herbert. (1938). *The Philosophy of the Act.* Chicago: Chicago University Press.

Mead, George Herbert. (2002). *The Philosophy of the Present.* Amherst, NY: Prometheus.

Merton, Robert. (1957). *Social Theory and Social Structure: Revised and Enlarged Edition.* New York: Free Press.

Mihal, Jan. (2021). *Responding to the Over-Inclusiveness Objection to Hart's Theory of Law: A Causal Approach* (SSRN Scholarly Paper No. ID 3740353), https://papers.ssrn.com/abstract=3740353

Mihal, Jan. (2017). "Defending a Functional Kinds Account of Law." *Australian Journal of Legal Philosophy* 42: 121–44.

Miller, Seumas. (2019). "Social Institutions." In Edward N. Zalta (ed.), *The Stanford Encyclopedia of Philosophy* (Summer 2019 Edition). https://plato.stanford.edu/archives/sum2019/entries/social-institutions/.

Millikin, Ruth Garrett. (1999). "Historical Kinds and the Special Sciences." International Journal for Philosophy in the Analytical Tradition 95: 45–65.

Miotto, Lucas. (2021). From Angels to Humans: Law, Coercion, and the Society of Angels Thought Experiment. *Law and Philosophy* 40: 277–303.

Moor, Jaap A.de, and Wolfgang J.Mommsen (eds.). (1992). *European Expansion and Law: The Encounter of European and Indigenous Law in the 19th- and 2th-Century Africa and Asia.* 1st ed., Oxford: Berg.

Moore, Michael S. (1992). "Law as a Functional Kind." In Robert P. George (ed.), *Natural Law Theory: Contemporary Essays.* Oxford: Oxford University Press, 188–242.

Moore, Sally Falk. (1969). "Law and Anthropology." *Biennial Review of Anthropology* 6: 252–300.

Nekam, Alexander. (1967). "Aspects of African Customary Law." *Northwestern University Law Review* 62(1): 45–56.

Philips, Nelsen, Thomas B. Lawrence, and Cynthia Hardy. (2004). "Discourse and Institutions." *Academy of Management Review* 29: 635–52.

Pistor, Katharina. (2019). *The Code of Capital: How the Law Creates Wealth and Inequality.* Princeton: Princeton University Press.

Plato. (1991). *The Republic.* New York: Random House.

Postema, Gerald J. (2008). "Conformity, Custom, and Congruence: Rethinking the Efficacy of Law." In Matthew H. Kramer, Claire Grant, Ben Coburn, and Antony Hatzistavrou (eds.), *The Legacy of H.L.A.Hart: Legal, Political, and Moral Philosophy.* Oxford: Oxford University Press, 45–66.

Postema, Gerald J. (2015). "Jurisprudence, the Sociable Science." *Virginia Law Review* 101: 869–901.

Postema, Gerald J. (2021). "Philosophical Jurisprudence: A Vision." UNC Legal Studies Paper, SSRN: https://ssrn.com/abstract=3972708 or http://dx.doi.org/10.2139/ssrn.3972708

Pound, Roscoe. (1910) "Law in Books and Law in Action." *American Law Review* 44: 12–36.

Preston, Beth. (2018). "Artifact." In Edward N. Zalta (ed.), *The Stanford Encyclopedia of Philosophy* (Fall 2020 Edition). https://plato.stanford.edu/entries/artifact/

Priel, Dan. (2018). "Not all Law is an Artifact: Jurisprudence Meets the Common Law." In Luka Burazin, Ken Einar Himma, and Corrado Roversi (eds.), *Law as an Artifact*. Oxford: Oxford University Press, 239–67.

Priel, Dan. (2019). "Law as a Social Construction and Conceptual Legal Theory." *Law and Philosophy* 38: 267–87.

Raz, Joseph. (1979). *The Authority of Law: Essays on Law and Morality.* Oxford: Clarendon Press.

Raz, Joseph. (2009a). *Between Authority and Interpretation*, 2nd ed. Oxford: Oxford University Press.

Raz, Joseph. (2009b). *The Authority of Law*, 2nd ed. Oxford: Oxford University Press.

Roberts, Simon. (1976). "Law and the Study of Social Control in Small-Scale Societies." *The Modern Law Review* 39(6): 663–79.

Rotberg, Robert I. (2003). "Failed States, Collapsed States, Weak States: Causes and Indicators." In Robert Rotberg (ed.), *State Failure and State Weakness in a Time of Terror*. Washington, DC: Brookings Institution Press, 1–26.

Roughan, Nicole, and Andrew Halpin (eds.). (2017). *In Pursuit of Pluralist Jurisprudence*. Cambridge: Cambridge University Press.

Roversi, Corrado. (2015). "Legal Metaphoric Artifacts." In B. Brozek, J. Stelmach, and L. Kurek, (eds.), *The Emergence of Normative Orders*. Krakaw: Copernicus Center Press, 215–80.

Roversi, Corrado. (2018). "On the Artifactual – and Natural – Character of Legal Institutions." In Luka Burazin, Kenneth E. Himma, and Corrado Roversi (eds.), *Law as an Artifact*. Oxford: University Press, 89–111.

Roversi, Corrado. (2019). "Law as an Artefact: Three Questions." *Analisi E Diritto* 2019: 41–68.

Rowell, Arden. (2019). "Legal Knowledge, Belief, and Aspiration." *Arizona State Law Journal* 51(1): 225–92.

Sapolsky, Robert M. (2017). *Behave: The Biology of Humans at Our Best and Worst*. New York: Penguin Press.

Schauer, Frederick. (2005). "The Social Construction of the Concept of Law: A Reply to Julie Dickson." *Oxford Journal of Legal Studies*, 25: 493–501.

Searle, John R. (1995). *The Construction of Social Reality*. New York: The Free Press.

Searle, John R. (2006). "Social Ontology: Some Basic Principles." *Anthropological Theory* 6: 12–29.

Searle, John R. (2010). *Making the Social World: The Structure of Human Civilization*. New York: Oxford University Press.

Shapiro, Scott J. (2000). "Law, Morality, and the Guidance of Conduct." *Legal Theory* 6(2): 127–70.

Shapiro, Scott J. (2011). *Legality*. Cambridge, MA: Harvard University Press.

Simpson, A. W. Brian. (1986). *A History of Land Law*, 2nd ed. Oxford: Oxford University Press.

Smith, Adam. (1982). *Lectures on Jurisprudence* (R. L. Meeks, D. D. Raphael, and P. G. Stein eds.). Indianapolis, Indiana: Liberty Fund.

Tamanaha, Brian Z. (2001). *A General Jurisprudence of Law and Society*. Cambridge: Cambridge University Press.

Tamanaha, Brian Z. (2006). *Law as a Means to an End: Threat to the Rule of Law*. Cambridge: Cambridge University Press.

Tamanaha, Brian Z. (2017). *A Realistic Theory of Law*. New York: Cambridge University Press.

Tamanaha, Brian Z. (2021). *Legal Pluralism Explained: History, Theory, Consequences*. Oxford: Oxford University Press.

Thomassen, Amie L. (2014). "Public Artifacts, Intentions, and Norms." In Martin Franssen, Peter Kroes, Thomas A. C. Reydon, and Peter Vermas (eds.), *Artefact Kinds: Ontology and the Human Made World*. Dordrecht: Springer, 45–62.

Tollefsen, Deborah. (2002). "Collective Intentionality and the Social Sciences." *Philosophy of the Social Sciences* 32: 25–50.

Tomasello, Michael. (2104). *A Natural History of Human Thinking*. Cambridge, MA: Harvard University Press.

Tomasello, Michael. (2019). *Becoming Human: A Theory of Ontogeny*. Cambridge: Belknap Press.

Trigger, Bruce G. (2003). *Understanding Early Civilizations*. Cambridge: Cambridge University Press.

van den Bergh, G. C. J. J. (1969). "Legal Pluralism in Roman Law." *Irish Jurist (1966)* 4(2): 338–50.

van Rooij, Benjamin. (2020). *Do People Know the Law? Empirical Evidence about Legal Knowledge and Its Implications for Compliance* (SSRN Scholarly Paper No. ID 3563442), https://papers.ssrn.com/abstract= 3563442

Waldron, Jeremy. (1999). "All We Like Sheep." *Canadian Journal of Law and Jurisprudence* 12(1): 169–90.

Waldron, Jeremy. (2013). *International Law: "A Relatively Small and Unimportant" Part of Jurisprudence?* (SSRN Scholarly Paper No. ID 2326758), https://papers.ssrn.com/abstract=2326758

Waluchow, Wilt J. (2008). "Legality, Morality, and the Guiding Function of Law." In Matthew H. Kramer, Claire Grant, Ben Coburn, and Antony Hatzistavrou (eds.), *The Legacy of H.L.A. Hart: Legal, Political, and Moral Philosophy*. Oxford: Oxford University Press, 85–97.

Webber, Gregoire. (2015). "Asking Why in the Study of Human Affairs." *American Journal of Jurisprudence* 60(1): 51–78.

Weber, Max. (1978). *Economy and Society: An Outline of Interpretive Sociology*. (G. Roth and C. Wittich, eds.). Berkeley: University of California Press.

Wilson, Edward. (2012). *The Social Conquest of Earth*. New York: Liveright Publishing.

Winch, Peter. (1958). *The Idea of a Social Science and its Relation to Philosophy*. London: Rougtledge & Kegan Paul.

Woodman, Gordon R. (2011). "A Survey of Customary Laws in Africa in Search of Lessons for the Future." In Jeanmarie Fenrich, Paolo Galizzi, and Tracy Higgins (eds.), *The Future of African Customary Law*. Cambridge: Cambridge University Press, 9–30.

Yassari, Nadjma, and Mohammad Hamid Saboory. (2010). "Sharia and National Law in Afghanistan." In Jan Michiel Otto (ed.), *Sharia Incorporated: A Comparative Overview of the Legal Systems of Twelve Muslim Countries in Past and Present*. Amsterdam: Leiden University Press, 272–317.

About the Author

Brian Tamanaha is the John S. Lehmann University Professor at Washington University School of Law. He is the author of ten books on jurisprudence and law and society, which have collectively received six awards, including the 2019 IVR Book Prize for best book in Legal Philosophy. He has delivered eight endowed lectures around the world, including the Kobe Memorial Address in Tokyo and the Julius Stone Address in Sydney, and his work has been translated into twelve languages.

George Pavlakos
University of Glasgow

George Pavlakos is Professor of Law and Philosophy at the School of Law, University of Glasgow. He has held visiting posts at the universities of Kiel and Luzern, the European University Institute, the UCLA Law School, the Cornell Law School and the Beihang Law School in Beijing. He is the author of *Our Knowledge of the Law* (2007) and more recently has co-edited *Agency, Negligence and Responsibility* (2021) and *Reasons and Intentions in Law and Practical Agency* (2015).

Gerald J. Postema
University of North Carolina at Chapel Hill

Gerald J. Postema is Professor Emeritus of Philosophy at the University of North Carolina at Chapel Hill. Among his publications count *Utility, Publicity, and Law: Bentham's Moral and Legal Philosophy* (2019); *On the Law of Nature, Reason, and the Common Law: Selected Jurisprudential Writings of Sir Matthew Hale* (2017); *Legal Philosophy in the Twentieth Century: The Common Law World* (2011), *Bentham and the Common Law Tradition, 2nd edition* (2019).

Kenneth M. Ehrenberg
University of Surrey

Kenneth M. Ehrenberg is Reader in Public Law and Legal Theory at the University of Surrey School of Law and Co-Director of the Surrey Centre for Law and Philosophy. He is the author of *The Functions of Law* (2016) and numerous articles on the nature of law, jurisprudential methodology, the relation of law to morality, practical authority, and the epistemology of evidence law.

Associate Editor
Sally Zhu
University of Sheffield

Sally Zhu is a Lecturer in Property Law at University of Sheffield. Her research is on property and private law aspects of platform and digital economies.

About the Series

This series provides an accessible overview of the philosophy of law, drawing on its varied intellectual traditions in order to showcase the interdisciplinary dimensions of jurisprudential enquiry, review the state of the art in the field, and suggest fresh research agendas for the future. Focussing on issues rather than traditions or authors, each contribution seeks to deepen our understanding of the foundations of the law, ultimately with a view to offering practical insights into some of the major challenges of our age.

Cambridge Elements ≡

Philosophy of Law

Printed in the United States
by Baker & Taylor Publisher Services